Australian Edition

Getting Started in Property Investing

FOR DUMMIES®

A Wiley Brand

by Bruce Brammall
Eric Tyson
Robert S. Griswold

Getting Started in Property Investing For Dummies®
Australia Edition published by
Wiley Publishing Australia Pty Ltd
42 McDougall Street
Milton, Qld 4064
www.dummies.com

Copyright © 2013 Wiley Publishing Australia Pty Ltd

The moral rights of the authors have been asserted.

National Library of Australia Cataloguing-in-Publication data:

Author:	Brammall, Bruce.
Title:	Getting Started in Property Investing For Dummies/Bruce Brammall, Eric Tyson, Robert S. Griswold.
Edition:	Australian ed.
ISBN:	9781118396742 (pbk.)
Series:	For Dummies.
Notes:	Includes index.
Subjects:	Real estate investment — Australia. Real property — Australia.
Other authors/ contributors:	Tyson, Eric (Eric Kevin) Griswold, Robert S.
Dewey Number:	332.63240994

Cover image: © iStockphoto.com/alexsl

Typeset by diacriTech, Chennai, India

Printed in Singapore by
C.O.S. Printers Pte Ltd

10 9 8 7 6 5 4 3 2 1

Contents at a Glance

Table of Contents

Introduction

*W*elcome to *Getting Started in Property Investing For Dummies*, Australian Edition! We're delighted to be your tour guides. Throughout this book, we emphasise three fundamental cornerstones that we believe to be true:

- ✔ Property is one of the three time-tested ways for people of varied economic means to build wealth (the others are shares and small business). Over the long term, you should be able to make an annual return of around 7 to 9 per cent per year investing in real estate.

- ✔ Investing in real estate isn't rocket science but does require doing your homework. If you're sloppy with your legwork, you're more likely to end up with inferior properties or to overpay for a property. Our book clearly explains how to buy the best properties at a fair (even below-market!) price. (Although we cover all types of properties, our book concentrates on residential investment opportunities, which are more accessible and appropriate for non-experts.)

- ✔ Although you should make money over the long term investing in good real estate properties, you *can* lose money, especially in the short term. Don't unrealistically expect real estate values to increase every year. When you invest in real estate for the long term, which is what we advocate and practise ourselves, the occasional price declines should be merely bumps on an otherwise fruitful journey.

How This Book Is Different

If you expect us (in property spruiker fashion) to tell you how to become an overnight multimillionaire, this is definitely not the book for you. And please allow us to save you money, disappointment and heartache by telling you that such shysters are only enriching themselves through their grossly overpriced CDs and seminars, or are likely urging you into their property developments with funding from their related-party loans.

Getting Started in Property Investing For Dummies, Australian Edition, covers tried and proven real estate investing strategies that real people, just like you, use to build wealth. Specifically, this book explains how to invest in houses, units, apartments, small apartment blocks, commercial properties and raw (undeveloped) land. We also cover 'indirect' real estate investments such as real estate investment trusts (REITs) that you can purchase through the Australian Securities Exchange or a real estate managed fund.

The objective of our book is to give you the best crash course in property investing, so that, if you choose to make investments in properties, you may do so wisely and confidently.

Foolish Assumptions

Whenever authors sit down to write books, they have particular audiences in mind. Because of this, they must make some assumptions about who the reader is and what that reader is looking for. Here are a few assumptions we've made about you:

- ✓ You're looking for a way to invest in real estate but don't know what types of properties and strategies are best. (We'll show you.)

- ✓ You're considering buying an investment property, be it a house, a unit, an apartment or flat, a small apartment or unit complex or an office building, but your real estate experience is largely limited to renting an apartment or owning your own home.

- ✓ You may have a small amount of money already invested in real estate, but you're ready to go after more or bigger properties.

- ✓ You're looking for a way to diversify your investment portfolio.

If any of these descriptions hits home for you, you've come to the right place.

How This Book Is Organised

We've organised *Getting Started in Property Investing For Dummies*, Australian Edition, into four parts. Here's what you can find in each.

Part I: Understanding Real Estate as an Investment

In this part, we explain how property compares with other investments, how to determine whether you've got what it takes to succeed as a real estate investor, and how much money you'll need to invest in various types of real estate. We cover why your home isn't really an investment property and why a holiday home can be both home and investment property. We also discuss the range of real estate investments available to you — such as residential and commercial properties — and researching property trusts.

Part II: Financing: Raising Capital and Sourcing Loans

You can't play if you can't pay. This part details how and where to come up with the dough you need to buy property. We explain the common loans available and some not-so-common ways to finance property investment. We also share all of our favourite strategies for finding and negotiating the best deals when you need a mortgage.

Part III: Finding and Operating Properties

This part looks at the rules of buying real estate right. We tell you how to determine where and what to buy. In this part, you find out how to choose the best locations and how to project a property's cash flow. We also take a look at the ongoing costs of real estate and what you need to consider to cover those expenses. Importantly, we also focus on the basics of being a landlord, and how to find and keep the best tenants and sign solid lease contracts. And finally, we provide some tips on building a property portfolio, as you look at purchasing your third (fourth, fifth, sixth . . .) real estate investment.

Part IV: The Part of Tens

This part contains ten important tips that didn't fit neatly into the rest of this book. This section includes ten ways to increase a property's return, from raising rent prices, to subdividing and developing, and taking advantage of tax benefits.

Icons Used in This Book

Throughout this book, you can find friendly and useful icons to enhance your reading pleasure and to note specific types of information. Here's what each icon means:

 This alerts you to those who may have conflicts of interest or offer biased advice, as well as other concerns that could really cost you big bucks.

 This icon flags concepts and facts that we want to ensure you remember as you make your real estate investments.

 Included with this icon are complex examples and interesting technical stuff that you may want to read to become even more familiar with the topic.

 This icon points out something that can save you time, headaches, money or all of the above!

 Here we're trying to direct you away from blunders and errors that others have made when investing in property.

 Suddenly investing in real estate is much easier with research tools a mouse click away. This icon highlights the most useful sites.

Where to Go from Here

If you have the time and desire, we encourage you to read this book in its entirety. It provides you with a picture of how to maximise your returns while minimising your risks in the property market. But you may also choose to read selected portions. That's one of the great things (among many) about *For Dummies* books. You can readily pick and choose the information you read based on your individual needs.

Part I
Understanding Real Estate as an Investment

Glenn Lumsden

'... and if the real estate market ever nosedives, you can always just live off the gingerbread.'

In this part ...

*R*eal estate is just one of many available investment options, so, in this part, we compare real estate investing with alternatives you may consider and look at how to fit real estate into your overall financial plans.

Chapter 1

Stacking Up Real Estate Against Other Investments

*T*he vast array of choices available to Australians is both a privilege and a burden. Go to the supermarket in search of something as simple as bread and you'll know exactly what we mean. Choice is even more widespread when it comes to the world of investment. You have thousands of choices among managed funds, shares, bonds ... the list is seemingly endless.

Allow us to help you through a portion of the cluttered world of investment. In this chapter, we start to explain how, why, when and where to invest successfully in real estate. And, even though we're advocates for investing in real estate, we also take you through some issues to weigh up if you're wondering whether you have what it takes to make money *and* be comfortable investing in real estate. We share our experiences, insights and thoughts on the long-term strategy for building wealth through real estate that, at its core, is a fundamentally simple investment strategy that virtually everyone with a long-term time frame and determination can understand and achieve.

Getting Yourself Motivated

It's never too early or too late to formulate your own plan into a comprehensive wealth-building strategy. For many, such a strategy can help with the challenges of funding private school education for children and ensuring a comfortable retirement. The stock market and other diversified investments are essential to a proper asset-allocation and diversification strategy.

The challenge involved with real estate is that it takes some real planning to get started. Without doubt, calling a stockbroker and purchasing a few shares in your favourite company is a lot easier than purchasing your first rental property. But buying good property is more time-consuming than difficult. You just need a financial and real estate investment plan, a lot of patience and the willingness to do some research and legwork, and you're on your way to building your own real estate empire!

The vast majority of people who don't make money in real estate make easily avoidable mistakes, which we help you steer clear of.

In this chapter, we give you some information that can help you decide whether you have what it takes to make money and be comfortable with investing in real estate. Unlike almost any other type of investment, real estate is hands-on. When you own shares in a company, you can't personally dictate how that company operates, or influence how profitable it is. Direct investment in property is the opposite. You're in control. Major decisions are in your hands. You can determine how to lift your income and how to raise your profits (or capital gains or equity). We compare real estate investments with other investments you may be considering. We provide questions you need to ask yourself before making decisions. And, finally, we offer guidance on how property can fit into your overall personal financial plans.

As Bruce approached the end of his 20s, his employment as a business journalist gave him the scope to investigate how the rich made their money. He found that he could usually narrow down the stories behind a person's wealth to a few themes — inventing something, owning and running a business, or successfully investing in other businesses. These businesspeople and investors covered a variety of industries and their business successes had no obvious common link. However, a non-business link soon emerged. Most of these people seemed to have made substantial sums of money from property investment.

Comparing Real Estate with Other Investments

You've surely heard about or even considered many different investments over the years. To help you appreciate and understand the unique attributes of real estate, we compare real estate with other wealth-building investments like shares and running your own business, using key economic attributes.

Returns

Clearly, a major reason many people invest in real estate is for the healthy *total returns* (which can include both ongoing income and the capital appreciation of the property). Real estate generates robust long-term returns because, like shares and small business, it's an ownership investment. By that, we mean that real estate is an asset that has the ability to produce income *and* capital growth.

Our research and experience suggest that total real estate investment returns are comparable to those from shares (about 7 to 10 per cent annually, measured over decades). (In Chapter 2, we discuss *real estate investment trusts* (REITs), which are publicly traded companies that invest in commercial real estate such as apartment buildings, office complexes, shopping centres and so on. These have gone through considerable periods of growth, with rates of greater than 10 per cent growth, though returns since the onset of the global financial crisis (GFC) have been sorely tested.)

And *you* can earn returns better than 10 per cent per year if you select excellent properties in the best areas and manage them well. That said, investing in real estate is accompanied by the following:

> ✔ **Few knockout wins:** Your returns from real estate probably won't approach the knockout wins that are sometimes achieved by business entrepreneurs or by picking penny-dreadful shares on the stock market and doubling your capital in a month. Real estate profits take time — profits are earned through hard work, judgement and research.

✔ **Ups and downs:** You're not going to earn a 7 to 10 per cent return every year. Although you have the potential for significant profits, owning real estate isn't like owning a licence to print money. Like stocks and other types of ownership investments, real estate goes through down as well as up periods. Most people make money in real estate by holding property over many years.

✔ **High transaction costs:** If you buy a property and then want out a year or two later, you may find that, even though the property has appreciated in value, much (if not all) of your profit has been wiped away by the high transaction costs. Typically, the costs of buying and selling — which include stamp duty, real estate agent commissions, loan fees, property taxes and other settlement costs — amount to about 10 per cent of the purchase (or selling) price of a property. So, although your property might appreciate 10 per cent in value in a short time, costs and taxes can mean you may have had a greater return if you'd stashed your money in a bank account for that period.

✔ **Tax implications:** Last, but not least, when you make a profit on your real estate investment, the Australian Taxation Office (ATO) is waiting with open hands for their share. So, throughout this book, we highlight ways to improve your after-tax returns.

Risk

Real estate doesn't always rise in value. That said, market values for real estate don't usually suffer from as much volatility as share prices do. The excitement in global share markets leading up to November 2007 saw many countries' stock markets double, or more, in value from 2003. Australia's stock market rose from around 2,700 points to a high above 6,800 points. Then the global debt bubble burst, which panicked investors globally and led to the GFC. Australia's market fell all the way to below 3,100 points — back almost to where its run had started. You're far less likely to see that kind of roller-coaster experience with real estate market values. The reason is land — even if the building is removed from a piece of land, the land itself generally retains its value. With an apartment block, the value of the land might be as little as 10 per cent of the full purchase price. For some houses, the value of the land could be as much as 70 per cent.

How leverage affects your real estate returns

Real estate is different from most other investments in that you can borrow (finance) the entire cost of the asset, plus all of the significant associated purchase costs (such as stamp duty and settlement costs) if you have sufficient equity in other assets. The loan can often amount to as much as 106 or 107 per cent of the actual purchase cost of the house, depending on which state it's in and the costs associated with the purchase. Therefore, you can use a small deposit to buy, own and control a much larger investment. So, when your real estate increases in value (which is your aim), your returns are leveraged to take into account your total investment (your own deposit, plus the borrowed amount).

Take a look at this simple example. Suppose that you purchase a property for $400,000 and pay a $40,000 deposit. Over the next three years, imagine that the property appreciates 20 per cent to $480,000. Thus, you have a profit (on paper) of $80,000 ($480,000 minus $400,000) on an investment of just $40,000. In other words, you've made a 200 per cent return on your investment. (*Note:* This example ignores cash flow — whether your expenses from the property exceed the rental income that you collect or vice versa — and the tax benefits associated with rental real estate.)

But don't forget that leverage magnifies all of your returns and those returns aren't always positive! If your $400,000 property decreases in value to $360,000, even though it has only dropped 10 per cent in value, you actually lose (on paper) 100 per cent of your original $40,000 investment. See 'Income- and wealth-producing potential' later in this chapter for a more detailed example of investment property profit and return.

Keep in mind, though (especially if you tend to be concerned about shorter term risks), that certain types of real estate in some areas can suffer from declines of 10 to 20 per cent, or more. If you make a deposit of, say, 20 per cent and want to sell your property after a 10 to 15 per cent price decline, after you factor in transaction costs, you may find that all (as in 100 per cent) of your invested dollars are wiped out. So you can lose everything.

You can greatly minimise your risk in property investment through buying and holding property for many years (seven to ten or more).

Liquidity

The ease and cost with which you can sell and get your money out of an investment — known as *liquidity* — is one of directly held real estate's shortcomings. Real estate is relatively illiquid: You can't sell a piece of property with the same speed as you can whip out your ATM card to withdraw money from your bank account, or sell some shares with a phone call or a click of your computer's mouse. You also can't sell part of a house, although you can sell part of a shareholding.

We actually view property's lack of liquidity as a strength, certainly compared with stocks that people often trade in and out of because doing so is so easy and seemingly cheap. As a result, many stock market investors tend to lose sight of the long term and miss out on the bigger gains that accrue to patient buy-and-hold investors. Because you can't track the value of investment real estate daily on your computer, and because real estate takes considerable time, energy and money to sell, you're far more likely to buy and hold properties for the longer term.

Income- and wealth-producing potential

Compared with most other investments, real estate can excel at producing income for property owners. So, in addition to the longer term appreciation potential, you can also earn income year in, year out. Real estate can be both a true growth and income investment.

The growth in value of your properties compounds over years of holding them. The best part about capital growth is that you don't have to pay any tax on it until you sell the property and pay capital gains tax (CGT), unlike any positive income from the property, on which you have to pay tax each year.

If you have property that you rent out, you have money coming in every month in the form of rent. When you own investment real estate, you also incur costs that include your mortgage payment, agent fees, land tax, insurance and maintenance. It's the interaction between incoming revenue and outgoing expenses that tells you whether you're positively geared or negatively geared.

For income tax purposes, you also get to claim an expense that isn't really an out-of-pocket cost — *depreciation*. Depreciation enables you to reduce your income tax bill and hence increase your cash flow.

Unless you make a large deposit, a positively geared property may be difficult to achieve in the early years of ownership. During soft periods in the local economy, rents may rise more slowly than your expenses (rents may even fall). That's why you must ensure that you can weather financially tough times. In the worst cases, we've seen rental property owners lose both their investment property and their homes. See the section 'Fitting Real Estate into Your Financial Plans' later in this chapter.

Over time, your net rental income, which is subject to ordinary income tax, should rise as you improve the property and increase your rental prices faster than the rate of increase for your property's overall expenses. What follows is a simple example to show why even modest rental increases are magnified into larger positive incomes and healthy returns on investment over time.

Suppose that you're in the market to purchase a family home that you want to rent out and that such properties are selling for about $500,000 in the area you've deemed to be a good investment. (*Note:* Housing prices vary widely across different areas but the following example should give you a relative sense of how a rental property's expenses and revenue change over time.) You expect to make a 20 per cent deposit and take out an interest-only mortgage (at an initial rate of 7.5 per cent) for the remainder of the purchase price — $400,000. Here are the details:

Monthly mortgage payment	$2,500
Other monthly expenses (maintenance, insurance and so on)	$300
Monthly rent	$1,250

In Table 1-1, we show you what happens with your investment over time. We assume that your expenses (except for your mortgage payment, which we assume averages out at your initial rate) increase 4 per cent annually and your rent stays a static 3 per cent of the value of the property. We also assume that your property appreciates at 6 per cent per year. (For simplification purposes, we've ignored depreciation in this example. If we had included the benefit of depreciation, it would further enhance the calculated returns.)

Table 1-1	How a Rental Property's Income and Wealth Build over Time			
Year	Monthly Rent	Monthly Expenses	Property Value	Mortgage Balance
0	$1,250	$2,800	$500,000	$400,000
5	$1,672	$2,865	$669,100	$400,000
10	$2,238	$2,944	$895,400	$400,000
20	$4,008	$3,157	$1,603,500	$400,000
25	$5,364	$3,300	$2,145,900	$400,000

Now, notice what happens over time. When you first bought the property, the monthly rent was below the monthly expenses. By year 10, the gap has reduced considerably. At around year 15, income equals expenses. By year 20, income exceeds expenses by around $850 a month. Consider why this increase in income happens. Your largest monthly expense, the mortgage payment, will rise and fall roughly in line with official interest rates (but for the purposes of this example, we assume that it has averaged the same rate of 7.5 per cent over the period). Rent is likely to stay a relatively stable percentage of the value of the property, and we assume a 3 per cent rental return. So, even though expenses increase by 4 per cent per year, the compounding of rental inflation begins to produce larger and larger positive cash flow to the property owner. By around year 15, the asset is paying its own way — that is, it has moved from being negatively geared to being positively geared.

The real story, however, is in the Property Value column of Table 1-1. While the net income from the investment has been negligible, the property has continued to increase in value. At the end of 25 years, the property has appreciated by more than $1.6 million! Granted, $1.6 million in 25 years' time is not going to have the same purchasing power as $1.6 million now but, combined with a positive income from the property, here is an asset that has some real value. (And remember, if you factor in the tax deductions for depreciation, your cash flow and return would be even higher.)

In choosing an interest-only mortgage option, a debt of $400,000 is still attached to the property, which is the most tax-effective way to hold investment property if you still have other debts that are not tax-deductible (such as a home loan). But your equity in the house could be further improved if you change the loan from interest-only to principal and interest when the net income turned positive in about year 15.

Capital requirements

Although you can easily get started with traditional investments such as shares and managed funds with a few hundred or thousand dollars, the vast majority of quality direct real estate investments require far greater investments — usually tens of thousands of dollars. (We devote an entire part of this book — Part II, to be precise — to showing you how to raise capital and secure financing.)

If you don't have that kind of money burning a hole in your pocket, don't despair. We present you with lower cost real estate investment options. Among the simplest low-cost real estate investment options are real estate investment trusts (REITs). You can buy these like shares or you can invest in a portfolio of REITs through a managed fund (see Chapter 2 for more on property trusts).

Diversification value

An advantage of holding investment real estate is that its value doesn't necessarily move in tandem with other investments, such as shares or small-business investments. You may recall, for example, the share market moved sideways between early 2000 and early 2003. In 2000, however, real estate values on the east coast of Australia had been rising for about four years and continued rising for a few more years (until about 2003). In March 2003 — about 6 to 12 months before east coast properties levelled out — share prices started to take off again in a boom that ran through to late 2007, before crashing with the onset of the GFC. Property grew strongly from 2005, nationally, until 2010, when property prices started to decline across the country.

Real estate prices and share prices *can* move down together in value. Sluggish business conditions and lower corporate profits can depress prices for both shares and property.

Ability to add value

With shares in a company listed on the stock market, you're usually a small owner of a large company and your ability to make actual improvements to the company or its business is limited. With your own rental property, however, the biggest hurdle to improving your property is your budget and your imagination. You're in control of your property and, therefore, have the opportunity to improve the property to make it more valuable. You can fix up a property or develop it to allow you to raise rents. Perhaps through legwork, persistence and good negotiation, you can purchase properties below fair market value.

Persistent and savvy real estate investors can more easily buy property in the private real estate market at below fair market value. You can do the same in the stock market, but the scores of professional, full-time money managers who analyse share markets make finding bargains more difficult. We help you identify properties that you can add value to in Part III.

Tax advantages

Real estate investment offers numerous tax advantages. In this section, we contrast investment property tax issues with those of other investments.

Deductible expenses

Owning a property has much in common with owning your own small business. Every year, you account for your income and expenses on a tax return. We can't stress too strongly the need to be diligent about your bookkeeping. If you're not prepared to learn how to file properly (or pay someone to do it for you), property investment may not be for you. At a minimum, you need to have a folder for the longer term documentation for each property you own and another system for ongoing items.

Depreciation and capital works allowances

Two types of expense that you get to deduct for rental real estate on your tax return don't necessarily actually involve spending money. The first is *depreciation*, which is an allowable tax deduction that's essentially an acceptance that parts of the investment property have a finite life span and will need replacement one day. These depreciable items are largely fixtures and fittings. The second deduction is the *capital works allowance*, often referred to as the *building* or *capital depreciation allowance*, which is a special write-off for structural costs. This book uses the more common term of *building depreciation*.

Buildings, technically, can last for hundreds of years. However, the Tax Office allows buildings built after September 1985 to be 'depreciated' (at various rates), allowing investors to claim an annual cost until the building, for taxation purposes, is worth zero (in most cases, that will be 40 years after it was built). The other sort of depreciation is for fixtures, fittings and other items that largely will have to be replaced — for example, every 5, 10 or 15 years.

Negative-gearing losses

Unlike some countries, at the time of writing, Australian tax law doesn't limit deductions for income losses made on investments being applied to regular income. This is partly why property investors are fans of negative gearing.

If, according to the accounting treatment of your investment, your property 'lost' $15,000 for one year, you can write that off against the income you earn from your day job. So, if you earned $70,000 from your full-time job, but your property was negatively geared to the tune of $15,000, you have to pay income tax on only $55,000 ($70,000 − $15,000).

Sure, you've lost $15,000 on your investment but, if your property has increased in value by, say, $20,000 or more, you're ahead, possibly on several fronts, because of the way properties are taxed differently for income versus capital gains.

Halving of capital gains tax

Capital gains tax (CGT) has been tinkered with many times since it was introduced in the 1980s. Assets owned prior to 19 September 1985 are exempt from CGT. Any investment purchased after that date is a CGT asset, and tax is likely to be required to be paid on profits.

The most recent significant changes to CGT occurred in 1999. In a nutshell, any asset held for longer than a year qualifies for a 50 per cent reduction in the gain itself, before it's added to other income to be taxed. Because property is an asset that usually requires a longer holding period, property owners tend to benefit from this change more so than share owners.

Determining Whether Investing in Real Estate Is for You

We believe that most people can succeed at investing in real estate if they're willing to do their homework, which includes selecting top professionals to work with. In the sections that follow, we ask several important questions to help you decide whether you have what it takes to succeed and be happy with real estate investments that involve managing property.

Do you have sufficient time?

Purchasing and owning investment real estate and being a landlord is time-consuming. If you fail to do your homework before purchasing property, you can end up overpaying or buying real estate with a mass of problems. Finding competent real estate professionals takes time. Investigating suburbs also soaks up plenty of hours (information on performing this research is located in Chapter 6).

As for managing a property, you can do it yourself, but that also takes time. Usually, hiring a good local real estate agent will save you time and money in the long term.

 If you're stretched too thin due to work and family responsibilities, real estate investing may not be for you. You may wish to look into the less time-intensive real estate investments discussed in Chapter 2.

Can you deal with problems?

Challenges and problems inevitably occur when you try to buy a property. Purchase negotiations can be stressful and frustrating. You can also count on some problems coming up when you own and manage investment real estate. Most tenants won't care for a property the way property owners would.

If every little problem (especially those you think may have been caused by your tenants) causes you distress, at a minimum, you should only own rental property with the assistance of a property manager. You should also question whether you're really going to be happy owning investment property. The financial rewards come well down the road, but you'll be living any day-to-day ownership headaches immediately.

Can you hire and fire?

Even extensive research of the people you employ to help you with your property investments can't create perfect relationships. Sometimes your advisers (solicitors, agents, accountants and so on) will stuff it up. By the way, you will too. Accepting occasional problems is okay. But if problems persist and those errors continue to cost money, you have to be strong enough to sack your advisers.

Real estate agents, for example, can be an ongoing source of frustration. Typically, rental agency staff are younger and less experienced. If the service they deliver is constantly below that promised, you may need to sack them.

Does real estate interest you?

The best real estate investors have a curiosity and interest in real estate. If you don't already possess it, such an interest and curiosity *can* be cultivated — and this book may just do the trick.

People who have had success with stock market investing may be uncomfortable venturing into real estate investments. Others we know are on a mission to start their own business and may prefer to channel their time and money into that outlet.

But, even if you prefer other investments, you should consider the diversification value that real estate offers. When the stock market tanked in early 2008, property investors were grateful their holdings were appreciating in value and offsetting the fact that their stock market investments had turned sharply south.

Fitting Real Estate into Your Financial Plans

For most non-wealthy people, purchasing investment real estate has a major impact on their overall personal financial situation. So, before you go out to buy property, you should thoroughly examine your money life and be sure your fiscal house is in order. The following sections explain how you can do just that.

Ensure your best personal financial health

If you're trying to improve your physical fitness by exercising, eating junk food and smoking are going to be barriers to your goal. Likewise, investing in real estate or other growth investments, such as stocks, while you're carrying high-cost consumer debt (credit cards, car loans and so on) and spending more than you earn impedes your financial goals.

Before you set out to invest in real estate, pay off all your non-home-loan consumer debt. Not only will you be financially healthier for doing so, but you'll also enhance your future mortgage applications.

Eliminate wasteful and unnecessary spending (analyse your monthly spending to identify areas for reduction). This exercise enables you to save more and better afford your investments, including real estate. Live below your means. As Charles Dickens said, 'Annual income twenty pounds; annual expenditure nineteen, nineteen, six; result, happiness. Annual income twenty pounds; annual expenditure twenty pound ought and six; result, misery.'

Protect your property and yourself with insurance

Regardless of your real estate investment desires and decisions, only the foolish would enter into a property investment wealth-creation strategy without having comprehensive insurance for themselves and their major assets, including the following (in order of importance):

- ✔ **Home and contents insurance:** You want homeowner's insurance because it not only protects you against the financial cost caused by a fire or other home-damaging catastrophe, but also provides you with liability protection.

- ✔ **Excess liability insurance:** This relatively inexpensive coverage, available in million-dollar increments, adds on to the liability protection offered on your home, investment property and car, for protection against large claims should they be brought against you.

✔ **Income-protection insurance:** For most working people, their biggest asset is their future income-earning ability. Income-protection insurance replaces a portion of your employment earnings if you're unable to work for an extended period due to an incapacitating illness or injury.

✔ **Life insurance:** If loved ones are financially dependent upon you, term life insurance, which provides a lump-sum death benefit, can help to replace your employment earnings if you die.

Insurance is universally known as a 'grudge purchase'. However, having proper protection gives you peace of mind and financial security, so don't put off reviewing and securing needed policies.

Consider superannuation and property investment

Most working Australians have a superannuation account. And, due to how the money managers who run those super funds invest that money, most Australians have some of their super invested in property. More than 80 per cent of Australians' super invested in managed funds sits in *balanced* funds (where about 60 per cent is invested in growth assets and 40 per cent in income assets — see the following section). About 5 to 15 per cent of any given super fund is invested in commercial property — office, industrial and retail buildings.

Self-managed super funds (SMSFs) are also able to own property. One favourite way is for a self-managed super fund to hold the commercial property of a related business entity. Consider, for example, a sole trader — we've named him Michael — who owns a business called ABC. Michael also runs his own self-managed super fund and the super fund owns the premises that ABC operates from. ABC pays the super fund rent.

Super funds can also own residential investment property and, since 2007, SMSFs can borrow to invest in real estate. Since these changes, investing in real estate through a SMSF has grown exponentially. However, some strong restrictions exist on how the borrowings can be undertaken, and anyone considering a geared property investment inside a SMSF needs to talk with suitably qualified financial advisers, accountants and lawyers.

Think about asset allocation

With money that you invest for the longer term, you should have an overall game plan in mind. Financial advisers use phrases such as *asset allocation* and *diversification*. This allocation indicates what portion of your money you have invested in different types of investments, such as shares and real estate (growth assets), or bonds and cash (income assets).

A Warning on Statistics

Since the beginning of investing, the supporters of property and the supporters of share-based investments have been at war. The 'property versus shares' debate will, no doubt, be one that never ends. Blinkered proponents of either asset class will swear that theirs is *the* top long-term performer. And they'll have the studies to prove their argument.

This book doesn't enter that debate. So many different numbers can 'prove' both sides of the argument. Property and shares are both growth assets. They both have long-term total returns that (depending on which study you're looking at or which stage of the cycle you're comparing) are in the range of 8 to 10 per cent. In the case of property, that return is made up of rents and capital growth. With shares, the return is in dividends and capital growth.

We believe in both asset classes and believe that diversification is important for all investment plans.

Chapter 2

Covering the Landscape of Common Real Estate Investments

*I*f you lack substantial experience investing in real estate, you should avoid more esoteric and complicated properties and strategies. In this chapter, we discuss the more accessible and easy-to-master property options, from residential to commercial properties, vacant land and property trusts.

Investing in Residential Properties

Residential property can be an attractive real estate investment for many people. Residential housing is easier to understand, purchase and manage than most other types of property, such as office, industrial and retail property. If you're a homeowner, you already have some level of experience locating, purchasing and maintaining residential property.

If you've been in the market for a home yourself, you know that, in addition to freestanding (detached) houses, you can choose from numerous types of attached or multi-dwelling properties, including units, apartments and townhouses. In the following sections, we provide an overview of why some of these may make an attractive investment for you.

Freestanding houses

As an investment, *freestanding* houses usually perform better in the long run than attached housing, units or apartments. In a good real estate market, most housing appreciates, but traditional detached homes tend to outperform other housing types for the following reasons:

- ✔ Freestanding houses attract more buyers — most people, when they can afford it, prefer detached dwellings, particularly for the increased privacy (and space).

- ✔ Units and townhouses are less expensive and easier to build — and to overbuild. Because of this potential for surplus properties on the market, such property tends to appreciate more moderately in price.

- ✔ Land value is the major driver of property prices — the higher the land content, the more likely capital growth, and freestanding houses tend to have higher proportions of land content than attached housing.

Because freestanding houses are the most sought after, market prices for such dwellings can sometimes become inflated beyond what's justified by the rental income these homes produce. Detached houses are likely to produce lower rental yields (rent as a proportion of current value) than most other options, partly because the land has a lower rental value.

With a house, you (in conjunction with a property manager, if you hire one) are responsible for maintenance. You have to find the tradespeople and coordinate the work. Also recognise that, if you purchase a house with many fine features and amenities, tenants living in your property won't necessarily treat it with the same tender loving care that you might.

A primary rule of being a successful landlord is to let go of any emotional attachment to a property. But that sort of attachment on the tenant's part is favourable: The more tenants make your rental property their 'home', the more likely they are to return it to you in good condition — except for the expected normal wear and tear of day-to-day living.

Attached housing

As the cost of land around major cities has skyrocketed, packing more multi-dwelling units into a given plot of land keeps housing somewhat more affordable. Here, we discuss the investment merits of units, apartments and townhouses.

Apartments and units

When you purchase a flat or apartment, you're actually purchasing the airspace and interior surfaces of a specific unit as well as a proportionate interest in the common areas — the pool, tennis court, grounds, hallways, laundry and so on. Although you (or your tenants) have full use and enjoyment of the common areas, remember that the body corporate (the collective owners of all apartments in the block) actually owns and maintains the common areas, as well as the building structures themselves, including the foundations, outside walls and doors, roof, plumbing, electrical and other building systems. Before purchasing an apartment, review the body corporate governing documents to check what's considered common areas, and consider annual body corporate fees (see Chapter 7 for more on ongoing fees).

A unit, on the other hand, can be an attached or detached dwelling on a block of land, with shared common ground (such as driveways and gardens). For example, two, three or more dwellings that have been built on a single block of land.

Apartments and units do tend to produce higher yields than houses. Most bodies corporate deal with issues such as roofing and gardening for the entire building and receive bulk-buying benefits. *Note:* You're still responsible for maintenance that's needed inside your unit, such as servicing appliances and interior painting.

Although apartments may be somewhat easier to maintain, they tend to appreciate slower than houses and even units. This is in part because apartment blocks lack scarcity value.

Townhouses

Essentially attached homes, *townhouses* are a hybrid between 'air space only' apartments and houses. Like apartments and units, townhouses are usually attached, typically sharing walls and a continuous roof. But townhouses are often two-storey buildings that come with a small courtyard and offer more privacy than an apartment.

As with apartments, it's extremely important that you review the body corporate governing documents before you purchase the property to see exactly what you legally own. Townhouses are usually organised so that no limitations are stipulated on the transferability of ownership of the individual lot that encompasses each dwelling and often a small area of immediately adjacent land or air space for a patio or balcony.

Apartment blocks

Apartment blocks tend to produce positive cash flow (rental income less expenses) in earlier stages of ownership. But, as with a house, the buck stops with you for maintenance of an apartment building. You can hire a property manager to assist you, but you'll still have oversight responsibilities (and additional expenses) in that event.

One way to add value, if zoning allows, is to convert an apartment block into strata-titled individual apartments. Keep in mind, however, that this metamorphosis requires significant research on the zoning front, some legal work to separate the titles, and possible remodelling and construction costs.

Deciding among the options

From an investment perspective, our top recommendations for first-time investors are houses or detached dwellings in developments of less than about four. We generally don't recommend apartments. If you can afford a smaller house instead of something with shared walls, buy the house.

Apartments make more sense for investors who don't want to deal with building maintenance and security issues. Avoid shared-wall dwellings (particularly apartments) in inner-city areas where the availability of prime development sites makes building many more apartment towers more likely. Apartment prices tend to perform best where nearby land has already been fully (or near fully) developed.

For higher returns, look for property where relatively simple cosmetic changes can allow you to raise rents, and so increase the market value of the property. Examples of such improvements may include, but aren't limited to:

- ✔ Adding fresh paint and floor coverings

- ✔ Improving the landscaping

- ✔ Upgrading the kitchen with new appliances and new cabinet and drawer hardware

All the preceding changes can totally change the look and feel of the property.

 Look for property with a great location and good physical condition but with some maintenance that the current owner has put off. Develop a hit list of items to achieve maximum results for minimum dollars — for example, a property with a large yard but dead grass, a two- or three-car garage but peeling paint or a broken door. Consider adding a remote garage door opener to jazz up the property for minimum cost. You might be surprised how much value you can add to a property owned by a burnt-out, absentee or totally uninterested owner who's tired of maintaining the property.

 Unless you can afford a large deposit (20 to 30 per cent or more), the early years of rental property ownership may financially challenge you, depending on the type of property:

- ✔ **Houses:** The early years of owning an investment property are usually the most difficult in which to achieve positive monthly cash flow, particularly with houses. The reason? Land value. Houses sell at a premium relative to the rent they command because the land itself has a lower rental value than the dwelling.

- ✔ **Apartments or apartment buildings:** Apartments and apartment buildings, particularly those with many units, occasionally produce a small positive cash flow, even in the early years of rental ownership.

With all properties, as time goes on, generating a positive cash flow gets easier because your mortgage expense stays loosely fixed (apart from interest rate fluctuations) while rents tend to increase faster than expenses. Regardless of what you choose to buy, make sure that you run the numbers on your rental income and expenses to see if you can afford the negative cash flow that often occurs in the early years of ownership.

Using Your Home as a Base for Investing

The first foray into property purchasing for most people is a home in which to live. In the following sections, we not only cover the advantages inherent in buying a home for your own use, but also explain why a home and an investment property are essentially mutually exclusive purchases (except in the case of holiday homes). We also cover the implications of converting your home to a rental property, as well as fixing it up and selling it. And we give you some pointers on how to profit from owning your own holiday home.

An important concept to understand is that a 'home' is not an 'investment property' from the perspective of investing. The two types of asset have too many differences, particularly when it comes to tax treatment, for them to be talked about as the same thing. As such, in this book, when you see the word 'home', we're talking about the dwelling in which you live (also known in tax terms as the principal place of residence). However, 'investment property' can pretty much cover any other property on which an income, usually rent, is earned.

Although a home is not an investment property, for most people their home is the basis from which most investment property is bought. The equity that has built up, for people who have owned their own home for a few years and have seen the value of their home grow and their loan reduce, becomes the cornerstone from which real wealth is built. The equity can be used as security for other investments in property and shares. Outside of a large cash deposit, banks see home equity as the best source of security for their customers to use to reinvest (we cover this in more detail in Chapter 3).

Why tax makes 'home' and 'investment' different

What separates the taxation treatment of homes from that of rented properties is the federal government's intention that the principal place of residence (home) should not be taxed, whereas investment properties should be taxed on the profits or income made in the same way that all other profitable investments are taxed.

The first major difference is capital gains tax (CGT) — a 'home' is generally exempt from CGT when sold. How much money you've made on your home doesn't matter. If the property has always been your home, you do not pay CGT on any profit you make. If you initially paid $50,000 for your home and you sell it for $2 million, you won't have to pay CGT — not a cent. Making the same profit on an investment property is a different story. You do have to pay CGT.

The second major tax difference between your home and an investment property is in the treatment of expenses incurred in relation to a property. Usually, expenses aren't tax-deductible for homeowners, but are deductible for an investment property. Tax deductibility makes a big difference to the real cost of an item. A homeowner who pays $200 to change the locks on his front door gets no deduction. But an investor who pays $200 for the same work can have up to $93 returned through tax (depending on the investor's marginal tax rate), which effectively reduces the cost of the same work to $107.

Buying a place of your own

During your adult life, you're going to need a roof over your head for many decades. You have two options: Either buy a place to live in yourself or pay someone else rent. Real estate is the only purchase or investment that you can either live in or rent out to produce income. Shares, bonds or managed funds can't physically provide a roof over your head!

Unless you expect to move within the next few years, buying a property to call home often makes good financial sense. Over the long haul, owning usually costs less than renting (loans reduce in real terms over time, while rents rise) and allows you to build *equity* (the difference between market value and loans against the property) in an asset.

Some commentators try to argue that your home is an investment property. Bruce strongly disagrees. When starting out in the world of property investment, you want to make the basic distinction between 'home' and 'investment property' (refer to the preceding section). Your home is somewhere for you to live — to 'stash your stuff' as an Australian comic once put it. It's a place to feel safe, to bring up a family, to relax, to create a lifestyle. An investment property is about making money. You're unlikely to ever live there.

You can briefly consider your home as part of your investment portfolio when you use that home as the cornerstone of your wealth-creation plans. It's usually the biggest single investment that you make. It's also usually responsible for creating equity that you can later use to make further investments (like buying investment properties). Many people move to a less costly home when they retire (known as *downsizing*). Downsizing in retirement frees up the equity you've built up over years of home ownership. You can use this money to supplement your retirement income and for any other purpose your heart desires.

How your home is similar to an investment is that your home usually appreciates in value over the years and you can use that money to further your financial goals. You can also turn your home into an investment property if you decide to move into another property. But at this point — particularly for tax purposes — the former home stops being a 'home' and becomes an 'investment property' and your new home gets the tax advantages and disadvantages of becoming your home.

Converting your home to a rental

Turning your current home into a rental property when you move is one way to buy and own more properties. Holding on to your current home when you're buying a new one can be advisable if you're moving into a larger home or moving interstate. This approach presents a number of positives:

- ✔ You save the time and cost of finding a separate rental property, not to mention the associated transaction costs.

- ✔ You know the property and have probably taken good care of it and perhaps made some improvements.

- ✔ You know the target market because the house appealed to you at an earlier stage of life.

Many people hold on to their current home for the wrong reasons when they buy another. This often happens in a depressed market — even though they're buying a new home at a lower price, at the same time they're facing the prospect of selling their former home for a reduced price. If you plan to move and want to keep your current home as a long-term investment property, you can. But turning your home into a *short-term* rental is usually a bad move because

> ✔ You may not want the responsibilities of being a landlord, yet you force yourself into the landlord business if you convert your home into a rental.
>
> ✔ You may have to pay some capital gains tax (CGT) — proportionate to the time you owned the property as an investment versus a home — on any profit when you sell.

 If you own a property as a home and then move interstate, for example, you may be able to hang on to it for as long as six years before you incur CGT, even if you put a tenant into the property. This law applies only if you don't claim another 'home' as a principal place of residence in the meantime.

 If you do convert your home into an investment property, you may be able to claim tax deductions for portions of the capital improvements that you made to the property while it was your home.

Diversifying away from home

One of the most important rules of investing is diversification. That's the mantra of 'don't put all your eggs in one basket'. Why? If you drop the basket, all your eggs break. However, if you spread your eggs among many baskets, you reduce the chance of breaking them all at once.

 The same rule holds true for property investment. Not only is it dangerous for someone to be invested solely in property, but investing exclusively in one geographical area is also dangerous. Most importantly, for first-time investors, that means buying in an area away from where you live.

If you own your own home, a good portion of your individual net wealth is affected by property prices in your neighbourhood. If your suburb sees a strong rise in values, that's great. It's not so great if your home falls in value. So what would happen if the only other major asset you owned was an investment property that you bought close to home? If the area continued to grow, fantastic. If it fell in value, you'd be in double trouble.

 Although time-consuming, investing in an area away from where you live isn't difficult. Begin by investigating suburbs on the other side of town or in an economy that relies on a different set of fundamentals. After you've had some experience in owning and running rental properties, you may even wish to further diversify your property holdings interstate.

Serial home selling

One strategy for investment is to move into each property you buy, renovate to add value to the place while you live there, and then sell in order to buy a new property. *Serial home selling* is about buying well-located 'renovator's delights', where you can invest your time, sweat and materials to make improvements that add more value than they cost. The advantage in serial home selling, of course, is that no CGT is payable on the family home. The major catch is that you must actually move into the property for a period. The length of time isn't prescribed by law, but the Australian Taxation Office (ATO) likes to see physical proof that the person has lived in the property.

Under this plan, the number of homes you can buy, do up and then sell over a lifetime is considerable — as long as you can prove to the ATO's satisfaction that you lived in the property.

Be sure to buy a home in need of that special TLC in a great neighbourhood where you're willing to live while you do up the place.

Here's a simple example to illustrate the potentially significant benefits of this strategy. You purchase a ramshackle renovator's delight for $400,000 that becomes your principal residence, and over the next 18 months you invest $50,000 in improvements (paint, landscaping, appliances, decorator items and so on). You also invest the amount of your time that suits your skills. You now have one of the nicer homes in the neighbourhood and you can sell this home for a net price of $600,000 after your transaction costs. With your total investment of $450,000 ($400,000 plus $50,000), your efforts have earned you a $150,000 profit completely tax-free. Thus, you've earned an average of $100,000 per year, which is not bad for a tax-exempt second income without strict office hours (although this example doesn't take into account stamp duty or agent selling costs).

Some cautions are in order when discussing serial home renovating and selling. The process is not for everyone. Bypass this strategy if any of the following apply:

- You're unwilling or reluctant to live through redecorating, minor remodelling or major construction.
- You're not experienced or comfortable with identifying undervalued property and improving it.

✔ You don't have the budget to hire a professional contractor to do the work, and you don't have the free time or the do-it-yourself (DIY) skills needed to enhance the value of the property.

One final caution: Beware of transaction costs. The expenses involved in buying and selling property — such as stamp duty, agent commissions and loan fees — can gobble into profits.

Holiday homes

A common way for people with the means to expand their real estate holdings beyond their primary home is to purchase a holiday home. For Australians, this expansion is usually a place by the beach, in the bush, or by a river or lake — a home in an area where they enjoy taking holidays.

Many people hope to own a holiday home and rent it out when they don't want to use it, for perhaps as much as 90 per cent of the year. They often believe that they can own this wonderful place of their own and, because they also lease it out, claim the whole thing as a tax deduction. Wrong! The ATO only allows you to claim tax deductions for the portion of the expenses that are related to the income-producing activity (that is, when it is truly available for rent). If you occupy it yourself for 15 weeks of the year, you can claim only the portion of expenses that represents 37 out of 52 weeks of deductions.

The downsides to holiday homes can be numerous, including the following:

✔ **Expenses:** You have nearly all of the costs of a primary home — mortgage interest, property taxes, insurance, maintenance, utilities and so on.

✔ **Property management:** Things can go wrong and you won't know. A pipe can burst, for example, and it may be days or weeks before the mess is found.

✔ **Lack of rental income:** Most people don't rent out their holiday homes, negating the investment property income stream that contributes to the returns real estate investors enjoy (refer to Chapter 1 for a comparison of real estate with other investments). If your second home is in a holiday area, you could rent out the property. However, this may entail all of the headaches of having many short-term renters.

Before you buy a second home, objectively weigh all the pros and cons. If you have a spouse or partner with whom you're buying the property, have a candid discussion. For most people, buying a holiday home is more of a consumption decision than it is an investment decision. That's not to say that you can't make a profit from owning a second home. However, your total potential investment returns shouldn't be the main reason you buy a second home. Don't forget to weigh up the value of your personal use versus the likely gains from income or capital gains (see Chapter 6 for more on buying property in holiday areas).

Considering Commercial Real Estate

Commercial real estate is a generic term that includes properties used for office, retail and industrial purposes. You can also include self-storage and hospitality (hotel and motel) properties in this category. Many Australians have turned a pub into both a successful business and a real estate holding.

Commercial real estate isn't our first recommendation, especially for inexperienced investors. Residential real estate is easier to understand and also usually carries lower investment and tenancy risks.

With commercial real estate, when tenants move out, new tenants nearly always require extensive and costly improvements to customise the space to meet their planned usage of the property. And you may have to pay for some of the associated costs in order to compete with other building owners. Fortunes can quickly change — small companies can go under, get too big for a space and so on. Change can be quick in the small business world.

So how do you evaluate the state of your local commercial real estate market? You must check out, for a number of years, the supply and demand statistics, such as how much total space (and new space) is available for rent, and how that has changed in recent years. What is the vacancy rate, and how has that changed over time? Also examine the rental rates, usually quoted as a price per square metre.

Uncovering Undeveloped Land

For prospective real estate investors who feel tenants and maintenance are ongoing headaches, buying undeveloped land may appear attractive. If you buy land in an area that's expected to experience expanding demand in the years ahead, you should be able to make a tidy return on your investment. This is sometimes referred to as *buying in the path of progress*, but the trick is to buy before it's obvious to all that new development is moving in your direction.

You may hit a winner if you identify land that others don't currently see as having value in holding for the future. However, identifying many years in advance which communities will experience rapid population and job growth isn't easy. Land in those areas that people believe will be the next hot spot already sells at a premium price, so getting ahead of the pack to find bargains takes a lot of research and usually a bit of luck. *Note:* You won't have much opportunity to get ahead of the curve and, if you guess wrong, you may need to hold on to some costly land for a long time!

Investing in land certainly has drawbacks and risks:

- ✔ **Care and feeding:** Land requires ongoing cash to pay the property taxes and insurances, with little or no income. Although land doesn't require much upkeep compared with tenant-occupied property, it almost always does require some financial feeding.

- ✔ **Opportunity costs:** Investing in land can be a cash drain. If you buy the land with cash, you have the opportunity cost of tying up your valuable capital (which could be invested elsewhere). Most likely, you put down up to 40 per cent in cash and finance the balance of the purchase.

- ✔ **Lack of depreciation:** You don't get the tax benefits of depreciation because land isn't depreciable.

On the income side, some properties may be able to be used for parking or storage.

Although large-scale land investment isn't for the entry-level real estate investor, savvy property investors have made fortunes taking raw land, getting the proper building approvals and then selling (or better yet, subdividing and then selling) the

parcels to developers. If you decide to invest in land, be sure
that you

✔ **Do your homework.** Ideally, you want to buy land in an
area that's attracting rapidly expanding companies and that
has a shortage of housing and developable land. Take your
time to really know the area.

✔ **Know all the costs.** Tally up your annual *carrying costs*
(ongoing ownership expenses such as property taxes)
so that you can see what your annual cash drain may
be. What are the financial consequences of this cash
outflow — for example, will you be able to fully fund it
from your ordinary income?

✔ **Determine what improvements the land may need.**
Running water, utility and sewer lines, building roads,
adding landscaping, and so on, all cost money. If you
plan to develop and build on the land that you purchase,
research these costs. Make sure you don't make these
estimates with your rose-tinted sunglasses on —
improvements almost always cost more than you expect
them to. (Check with the local council planning or building
department for their list of requirements.)

Also make sure that you have road access to the land.
Some people foolishly invest in landlocked properties.
When they discover that fact later, they think they can
easily get an easement for access, which may not be
the case.

✔ **Understand the zoning and environmental issues.** The
value of land is heavily dependent upon what you can
develop on it. Never purchase land without thoroughly
understanding its zoning status and what you can and
can't build on it. This advice also applies to environmental
limitations that may be in place or that could come into
effect without warning, diminishing the potential of your
property (with no compensation).

Some areas, particularly older suburbs with strong design
characteristics, have strong networks of local residents
who can organise themselves quickly to fight developments
and influence council officials. A change in zoning can be
a disaster for the value of a piece of land if its rating is
lowered.

Researching Property Trusts

Australia's love affair with property isn't confined to direct individual ownership — Australia is also one of the most advanced countries when it comes to property trusts. *Property trusts*, or real estate investment trusts (REITs), are collective vehicles where money is pooled to make investments. In Australia, the taxation implications of the property ownership usually flow through to unit holders of the trust. Property trusts come in two broad types: Those that are listed and publicly tradeable, and those that are unlisted and are, therefore, less liquid.

Property trusts are for-profit entities that own and operate different types of property, such as shopping centres, apartments, offices, warehouses, hotels and other rental buildings.

 Property trust managers typically identify and negotiate the purchase of properties that they believe are good investments, and manage these properties directly or through an affiliated advisory and management company, including all tenant relations. Thus, property trusts can be a good way to invest in real estate for people who don't want the hassles and headaches that come with directly owning and managing rental property.

Distinguishing between listed and unlisted property trusts

REITs are publicly tradeable, usually on the Australian Securities Exchange (ASX). For example, most Australians know of, or have shopped at, a Westfield shopping centre. The Westfield Group is one of the world's largest REITs and owns enormous quantities of commercial real estate in Australia, the United States and Europe.

 We recommend that investors not be shy about asking for full disclosure of the relationship between the property trust, its advisers and the management companies. Conflicts of interest often exist that aren't clearly disclosed; significant above-market fees may also need to be paid that ultimately reduce the cash flow and return on investment available for distribution.

Performing by the numbers

So what about performance? Over the long term, total returns from REITs are comparable to shares, and REITs tend to be less volatile. However, that's a 'general' principle that was recently broken. As global investment markets turned toxic in late 2007, REITs were actually ahead of the down trend. They started falling earlier and fell harder — REITs fell around 75 per cent during the 2007 to 2009 crash, while the Australian share market fell around 55 per cent. But REITs also had stronger recoveries when markets started coming to their senses in mid-2009 and 2010. In the context of an overall investment portfolio, REITs add diversification because their values don't always move in tandem with other investments.

One final attribute of REITs we'd like to highlight is the traditionally fairly substantial dividends, known as distributions, that REITs pay (although strong capital growth in the three years to early 2007 meant those yields fell).

Unlike direct real estate investments, investments in REITs are usually as easy to sell as shares. Although this can be a benefit, REITs also attract trigger-happy investors prone to making knee-jerk buying and selling decisions as they try to time the market or predict market trends.

You can research and purchase shares in individual REITs, which trade as securities on the major stock exchanges. Another way is to buy managed funds that invest in many property trusts. Some fund managers can charge 1 per cent per year in management fees. However, some index fund managers, such as Vanguard and Blackrock, charge as little as 0.24 per cent per year as a management fee.

In addition to providing you with a diversified, low-hassle real estate investment, REITs offer an additional advantage that traditional rental real estate doesn't. You can easily invest in REITs through a superannuation fund. As with traditional real estate investments, you can even buy REITs and managed funds invested in property with borrowed money. You can buy with as little as 25 per cent down (in some cases), using a margin loan, when you purchase such investments through a stockbroking account.

If investing in REITs, unlisted property trusts or property managed funds interests you, research is essential. You can do your own research by reading as much material as you can get your hands on, starting with the business and personal finance sections of major newspapers, plus the various finance-related magazines available online and from newsagents (or in some libraries). Alternatively, you can employ a reputable financial planner or adviser who has access to a number of research resources.

 With property managed funds, in addition to having a professional manager deciding what property trusts to buy and when, you enjoy consolidated financial reporting. If you purchase individual property trusts, listed or unlisted, you have to deal with tax statements for each and every trust you've invested in.

Part II
Financing: Raising Capital and Sourcing Loans

Glenn Lumsden

'The bank said we qualified for their special "one-piece-at-a-time" real estate investment loan. This is the first square metre.'

In this part ...

*I*n this important part, we detail the amount of money you need to get started and the best places to source those funds in the likely event that you'll need to borrow money for your real estate plans. We point out the key issues you need to consider in deciding the terms of your financing, because getting these steps right can help reduce the risk associated with the large debts that property investors inevitably have. We discuss traditional lending sources and the types of banking products that may aid your investment program.

As your portfolio grows, so will your debt and your reliance on good credit terms, so we detail how to make the most of your bank.

Chapter 3

Sources of Capital

*F*or many people, the trouble with real estate investing is that they lack the access to cash for the deposit. The old adage that 'it takes money to make money' is usually true in our experience. So how do you get started in real estate if you don't want to own distressed properties in the worst suburbs and you don't have a six-figure deposit to pay top dollar in the best suburbs? Successful real estate investing requires patience and a long-term vision. Our method of building real estate wealth over time is to create an investment portfolio that's sustainable and provides generous returns on your investments.

You don't necessarily have to be wealthy or have great savings to *begin* making attractive real estate investments. In this chapter, we present a wide range of funding options that offer something for virtually everyone's budget and personal situation.

Calculating the Costs of Entry

At some point in your life, you've surely had the experience of wanting to do something and then realising that you don't have sufficient money to accomplish your goal. Perhaps it was as simple as lacking the change to buy a chocolate bar as a child. Or maybe it happened on a holiday when you ran low on funds and tried to do business with a shop owner who took only cash when you carried only a credit card. No matter — the world of real estate investing is no different. You can't play if you can't pay.

Determining what you need to get started

Most of the time, real estate investors make a deposit and borrow most of the money needed to complete a purchase. That's the 'conventional way' to purchase investment properties and is likely to be the most successful method for you in the long run (as it has been for us).

For most residential investment properties, such as free-standing houses, semi-detached housing such as some townhouses and apartments, and even small multi-unit developments, you can gain access to good financing terms by making at least a 10 per cent deposit or offering significant equity (see the section 'What is equity?' later in this chapter). However, most banks in Australia charge lenders' mortgage insurance (LMI) when the size of the deposit (or equity guarantee) is less than 20 per cent. LMI is an exponential charge that increases as the deposit offered by the property buyer decreases. For more about LMI, see 'Overcoming deposit limitations' later in this chapter. (We also cover getting finance in Chapter 4, and delve into lenders' mortgage insurance more deeply in Chapter 5.)

A minimum deposit of at least 10 per cent is recommended for first-time property buyers. You can escape being charged LMI if you have a deposit (or equity) of at least 20 per cent.

You won't find such wonderful financing options for commercial real estate and raw land. Compared with residential properties, these types of investment properties usually require larger deposits and/or higher interest rates and loan fees.

Determining how much cash you need to close on a purchase is largely a function of the estimated purchase price. Here's an example: If you're looking at buying a modest house priced at $350,000, a 20 per cent deposit equals $70,000. You then add another 4 to 6 per cent for settlement costs (including stamp duty, title-transfer fees, bank fees and legal fees — see 'Overcoming deposit limitations' later in this chapter) to reach the estimated deposit of $98,500 that you would need to get the best financing options.

Of course, if you have your heart set on buying a property that costs almost three times as much — say, a property with a $950,000 sticker price — you need to increase these amounts and have around $295,500 for the best financing options.

Don't forget stamp duty

After the actual cost of the property itself, the next biggest cost in buying properties in Australia is *stamp duty* — a generally nasty, big, regressive tax levied by state and territory governments. Each government charges stamp duty in a different way, and it's usually tiered so that lower valued real estate is charged less stamp duty as a proportion of the value of the property.

Stamp duty usually ranges from about 3 to 5.5 per cent of the value of a property (although above certain amounts it can be very close to 6 per cent). For example, at the time of writing, buying a $450,000 property in Victoria incurs a stamp duty of $22,070, whereas in Queensland (which applies the cheapest stamp duty) buying a $450,000 property incurs a stamp duty of $14,175.

For details of exactly how stamp duty is charged in your state or territory, contact your local state revenue office or department of treasury. The following list of website addresses can help you get started:

- ✔ **Australian Capital Territory:** www.revenue.act.gov.au/duties

- ✔ **New South Wales:** www.osr.nsw.gov.au

- ✔ **Northern Territory:** www.nt.gov.au/ntt/revenue

- ✔ **Queensland:** www.osr.qld.gov.au

- ✔ **South Australia:** www.revenuesa.sa.gov.au

- ✔ **Tasmania:** www.treasury.tas.gov.au

- ✔ **Victoria:** www.sro.vic.gov.au

- ✔ **Western Australia:** www.finance.wa.gov.au/cms/index.aspx

Many states offer stamp duty exemptions or reductions for first-time home buyers, seniors or retirees, and those on low incomes. These exemptions or reductions don't usually extend to investment properties. You can buy a property, live in it for a period of time (usually one year), and then turn it into an investment property. If you cheat on the rules and you're found out, you face stiff fines. We don't recommend that you try to squeeze what's usually only a few thousand dollars out of a government program that's rightly not aimed at lining the pockets of property investors.

One legal way a property investor can reduce stamp duty is to look at government incentives offered to the building industry. In many states, for example, stamp duty concessions apply to properties bought 'off-the-plan' — a property buyer pays stamp duty only on the proportion of the property already completed. Take, for example, a $450,000 house and land package that values the land at $200,000 and the building and improvements at $250,000. If the contract is signed when approximately 30 per cent of the building work has been completed, the investor — and home buyer as well — pays stamp duty on the value of the land ($200,000) plus the building works completed ($75,000, or 30 per cent of $250,000). Stamp duty is then charged on $275,000 rather than the $450,000 total cost of the property.

In some states, you may be able to delay the payment of stamp duty. Check with your state or territory's revenue department for more details.

Overcoming deposit limitations

Many people, especially when they make their first real estate purchase, are strapped for cash. In order to qualify for the most attractive financing, lenders typically prefer that your deposit be at least 20 per cent of the property's purchase price. In addition, you need to reserve money to pay for other settlement costs such as stamp duty, title-transfer fees and loan fees. (Banks usually require commercial property buyers to put up 30 per cent, plus costs, as a deposit.)

If you don't have 20-plus per cent of the purchase price, don't panic and don't get depressed — you can still own real estate. We've got some solutions:

   ✔ **Lenders' mortgage insurance:** Most lenders can still offer you a mortgage even though you may be able to put down only 5 to 20 per cent of the purchase price. These lenders are likely to require you to pay lenders' mortgage insurance

(LMI) for your loan. This insurance can cost many thousands of dollars and is designed to protect the lender, not you, if you default on your loan. When you do have at least 20 per cent or higher equity in the property, you can usually eliminate the LMI. (For more information about this insurance, see Chapter 5.)

✔ **Delayed gratification:** If you want to keep finance costs down, postpone your purchase. Plan to save harder to build up a nest egg to use to invest in your first rental property. For more tips on saving, see the section 'Make saving a habit' later in this chapter.

✔ **Thinking smaller:** Consider lower priced properties. Smaller properties and those that need some work can help keep down the purchase price. (We also discuss ways to get started in the section 'No Home? No Worries!' later in this chapter.)

A low-entry-cost option

For the ultimate in low entry costs, real estate investment trusts (REITs) are best. These stock exchange traded securities (which can also be bought through REIT-focused managed funds) can be bought into for as little as a few thousand dollars. REIT managed funds can often be purchased for $1,000 or less inside super funds. (Refer to Chapter 2 for more on investing in REITs.)

Strictly limiting: The zero-deposit loan

If you're really strapped for cash and don't have equity in your own home that you can call on or offer as security, don't start thinking you can overcome deposit limitations with a zero-deposit loan. The risks are simply too high. While the global financial crisis (GFC) and associated credit crisis wiped out many providers in this area, some fringe lenders still let you purchase with a very low deposit. If the only lenders that are willing to lend you money are providers you'd never previously heard of, be very careful (see 'Primary Sources of Finance: Lenders Big and Small' later this chapter). Don't give in to fast-talking salespeople or slick advertising to start your property investment portfolio without having at least saved some sort of a deposit. The risks of a property going backwards only increase the chance that your first property could send you bankrupt.

Rounding Up the Required Cash

Most successful real estate investors we know, including ourselves, started building their real estate investment portfolios the old-fashioned way — through saving money and then gradually buying properties over the years. Many people have difficulty saving money because they are simply unwilling to limit their spending. Easy access to consumer debt (via credit cards and car loans) creates huge obstacles to saving more and spending less. Investing in real estate requires self-control and sacrifice. Like most good things in life, you must be patient and plan ahead to be able to invest in real estate.

Make saving a habit

As young adults, some people are naturally good savers. Those who save regularly have usually acquired good financial habits from their parents. Other good savers have a high level of motivation to accomplish goals — retiring young, starting a business, buying a home, prioritising time with their kids and so on. Achieving such goals is much harder (if not impossible) when you're living payday to payday and worried about next month's bills.

 If you're not satisfied with how much of your monthly earnings you're able to save, you have two options (and you can take advantage of both):

✔ **Boost your income:** To increase your take-home pay, working more may be a possibility, or you may be able to take a more lucrative career path. We also believe in investing in your education. A solid education is the path to greater financial rewards and can lead to all of the great goals we discuss here. Education is a key not only to your chosen profession, but also to real estate investing.

✔ **Reduce your spending:** For most people, this is the path to increased savings. Analyse your spending first, then consider how you can cut back. Although the possibilities to reduce your spending are many, you and only you can decide which options you're willing and able to implement. If you need more help with this vital financial topic, check out *Sorting Out Your Finances For Dummies*, Australian Edition, by Barbara Drury (published by Wiley Publishing Australia).

Tap into other cash sources

Saving money from your monthly earnings will probably be the foundation for your entry into your real estate investing program. However, you may have access to other financial resources for deposits. Before we jump into these, we offer a friendly little reminder: Monitor how much of your overall investment portfolio you place into real estate and how diversified and appropriate your holdings are, given your overall goals (refer to Chapter 1 for more guidance).

As you gain more comfort and confidence as a real estate investor, you may wish to redirect some of your dollars from other investments — such as shares, bonds and managed funds — into property. If you do, be mindful of the following:

✔ **Diversification:** Real estate is one of the prime investments (the others being shares and small business) for long-term appreciation potential. Be sure that you understand your portfolio's overall asset allocation and risk when making changes. Check out Chapter 1 for more details.

✔ **Tax issues:** The effective maximum federal government tax rate for long-term capital gains (investments held for more than 12 months and sold for a profit) is 23.25 per cent, due to the 50 per cent reduction in the gain itself. Investors in the two lowest income tax brackets may pay zero or 9.5 per cent tax on capital gains.

Primary Sources of Finance: Lenders Big and Small

When the Hawke–Keating federal government deregulated the banking system in the mid-1980s, the number of lenders in Australia exploded, as did the competition between them. But banks aren't the only institutions that lend money for investment property in Australia. Alternative mainstream lenders include building societies, credit unions, non-bank lenders and non-conforming lenders.

In the following sections we describe the different types of mainstream lenders that you can approach to finance property investment, and briefly cover how they operate. We advise property investors to stick with the mainstream lenders.

Banks

Traditionally, banks are deposit-taking institutions. They accept deposits from some customers and then lend this money to other customers. Because they're the backbone of the Australian financial system, banks are heavily regulated by federal government entities, including the Australian Prudential Regulatory Authority, the Australian Securities and Investments Commission, and the Reserve Bank of Australia.

When Australians think of banks, most call to mind the 'big four': The Australian and New Zealand Banking Group (ANZ, at www.anz.com), the Commonwealth Bank of Australia (CBA, at www.commbank.com.au), the National Australia Bank (NAB, at www.nab.com.au) and Westpac Banking Corporation (Westpac, at www.westpac.com.au). Between them, these banks account for more than 80 per cent of all banking transactions in Australia.

The big four aren't the only banks in Australia. Most states have at least one or two other banks, many of which are also expanding beyond their traditional state boundaries. These include the Bank of Queensland (www.boq.com.au) and Suncorp-Metway (www.suncorp.com.au) in Queensland, Bendigo and Adelaide Bank (www.bendigoadelaide.com.au) in Victoria and South Australia, and BankWest (www.bankwest.com.au) in Western Australia (owned by the Commonwealth Bank of Australia).

The foreign banks with significant presences in Australia include HSBC (www.hsbc.com.au), Citibank (www.citibank.com.au) and ING (www.ing.com.au).

For information on the different types of interest rates and the types of mortgages you're likely to be offered if you approach a bank to finance your property investment, see Chapter 4.

Building societies and credit unions

Prior to the mid-1980s, building societies and credit unions were the places you went to for a loan when the banks knocked you back. These institutions charged higher interest rates than the banks to cover the bigger risks they were taking to provide mortgages.

Today, most building societies and credit unions offer interest rates that rival their larger banking competitors' rates and tend to differentiate themselves by providing customised service. Some operate on a statewide or even national scale, but the majority are regionally based and extend to fewer than a handful of branches. However, through the power of the internet, many are able to offer loans nationally.

Non-bank lenders

The deregulation of the banking system in the 1980s eventually paved the way for non-bank lenders to become mainstream. The first and most successful of these is Aussie Home Loans (www.aussie.com.au), which arrived in time to ride the first big wave of anti-bank sentiment (generated by branch closures and sacking of staff to make higher profits) in the 1990s and undercut the banks' interest rates.

 As well as Aussie Home Loans, other small and nimble providers have also entered the market to offer an array of loans in recent years. Some have the reputation of being a little fly-by-night, often appearing attractive because of very low interest rates. As a property investor, price shouldn't be everything in your decision of which lender to use, and using a well-established lender should be a priority.

The main difference between banks, building societies and credit unions on the one hand and non-bank lenders on the other is how they source the money they lend out to property buyers. The traditional lenders source most of their money from depositors, whereas the non-bank lenders raise their money from money markets — international investors seeking fixed-interest returns from reasonably secure investments, such as Australian mortgages. The credit crisis of recent years made it more difficult for some of these lenders to find suitable financing terms to get money to onlend to property buyers in Australia. As a result, this section of the market was squeezed, with many players withdrawing.

Non-conforming lenders

The emergence of non-conforming lenders is the most recent innovation in mainstream lending. Pioneers in this area include Liberty Financial (www.liberty.com.au) and Bluestone Mortgages (www.bluestone.com.au). These lenders emerged in the late 1990s, when a vacuum was created in the middle market between traditional lenders and solicitors' funds, which lend on property at lender-of-last-resort interest rates.

Non-conforming lenders use a method called *risk-based pricing* to set individual mortgage rates for their borrowers. That is, customers are charged an interest rate that reflects the risk they pose of defaulting on the mortgage. Non-conforming lenders' terms are aimed at borrowers who find it very difficult to get a loan from mainstream lenders because they may have failed to provide enough satisfactory paperwork to satisfy traditional lending criteria — for example, customers who have an impaired credit record, are self-employed or have jobs with irregular income streams, such as consultants, freelancers, professional sportspeople and actors. A non-conforming loan usually starts with a premium on the interest rate, but, as the borrower proves his or her ability to pay, the premium is reduced.

Here's an example: If the current interest rate charged by a bank is 8 per cent, the non-conforming lender may agree to lend the money based on an interest rate premium of, say, 4 percentage points. When the borrower gets his loan, he must pay an interest rate of 12 per cent for the first year. Assuming the borrower continues to meet all repayments, the lender will reduce the interest rate each year. Eventually, the borrower is able to refinance to a different lender at normal interest rates.

Borrowing Against Home Equity

Most real estate investors begin building their real estate portfolio after they have bought their own home. Tapping into your home's equity may be a good deposit source for your property investments.

The family home, therefore, tends to be the primary source of capital for those who have developed equity. Lending against property is the primary business of banks. Banks are comfortable doing so, because they've developed systems that allow them to judge the risks associated with lending to an individual or to a sector in general (and, as we discuss in Chapter 5, banks can take out lenders' mortgage insurance — or LMI — on you failing on your mortgage). Because the bank maintains the mortgage over a property, it's usually happy to lend against the value of that property, knowing that if problems eventuate, it can take possession of the house and sell it to recover any losses incurred.

What is equity?

Equity is the difference between the value of an asset and the loan secured against that asset. For example, a home valued at $600,000 that has a loan attached for $350,000 has 'equity' of $250,000. Equity can be built in a property in two ways: The first is by paying the loan down and the second is when the value of the asset increases.

Most people see their equity grow faster from asset price growth than from paying down the loan. For example, say a homeowner bought her house ten years ago. The house was bought for $300,000 with a $250,000 loan and is now valued at $600,000. The loan has been paid down to $200,000, meaning equity of $400,000 has been built from initial equity of $50,000. Home equity provides the best and the cheapest form of financing for subsequent investments in real estate because this is the asset that banks feel most comfortable lending against. Most banks would allow the homeowner to 'access' some of that equity to invest.

Now, say the homeowner found a $400,000 investment property she wanted to purchase. She would go to her bank and request approval for a loan, if she hadn't already received pre-approval. Often, the bank would approve the client for a facility so she could write a cheque for the deposit from a new investment loan, in this case probably 10 per cent, or $40,000. When settlement occurs (usually in 30, 60 or 90 days), the loan will convert to a new investment property loan, which may take in all the extras, such as stamp duty and settlement costs. This could mean the loan over the investment property is as much as 106 per cent of the property's value, or $424,000 (see the next section, 'The 110 per cent loan — borrowing the lot and then some', for more details).

The homeowner-cum-investor now has two loans to service — the original home loan of $200,000, which she has been paying for ten years, and the new investment property loan of up to $424,000, which she'll have to fund with the aid of rent from the tenant, tax savings (if applicable) and other income.

In many cases, particularly where more than 90 or 100 per cent of the property price has been borrowed and no other security except the investor's home is offered, the investment property loan, or a portion of the loan, will be a mortgage against the home. It may appear as a separate loan, but if the investor were ever to default on the investment property loan, the bank would have the power to take control of (and sell) both properties in order to recoup its loans.

The investor has two ways to prevent this. The first is to put up a substantial cash deposit of perhaps 5 to 20 per cent of the total purchase price. The other is to take out a non-recourse loan (for an explanation of recourse financing, see Chapter 4).

The banks' comfort in lending against the value of your home tends to extend to lending on investment properties as well. That is, most banks charge the same interest rate on an investment property as they do on your home loan. For example, if you're paying 7.5 per cent interest on your home, most banks will finance you at the same rate for your investment property. Banks understand property is a lower risk for them because they retain the security of the mortgage against the property.

If you fall outside the confines of what banks think are 'normal' credit risks, all is not lost. Australia's major banks have so much competition nowadays that you can generally find another lender who will offer you reasonably favourable terms (refer to the section 'Primary Sources of Finance: Lenders Big and Small' earlier in this chapter).

Some investors use a strategy of turning their original home into an investment property. However, you have a number of tax implications to take into account before considering this strategy.

Before you go running out to borrow to the maximum against
your home, be sure that you

- ✔ **Can handle the larger payments.** If you're going to borrow
  the maximum against your home, make sure that you're
  going to be able to service the higher mortgage payments
  that are likely to accompany that strategy. Excessive
  leveraging can be dangerous and could come back to haunt
  you! Refer to Chapter 1 for the big picture on personal
  financial considerations.

- ✔ **Understand the tax ramifications of all your alternatives.**
  Interest charged on a home mortgage is not tax-deductible,
  whereas the interest paid on investment borrowings
  generally is, even if the investment mortgage is secured
  against your home.

- ✔ **Fully comprehend the risks of losing your home to
  foreclosure.** The more you borrow for any reason, the
  greater the risk that you could lose the roof over your
  head to foreclosure should you not be able to make your
  mortgage payments.

The 110 per cent loan — borrowing the lot and then some

So, if banks are most comfortable — and, therefore, offer the
best interest rates — when they're lending against property in
which equity has been built, would they also be comfortable
lending against a person's home in favour of an investment
property? The answer is 'yes', as a general rule.

In fact, banks will often lend an investor more than the cost of
the investment property. That's right; they'll lend the cost of the
property, plus all the other incidental costs that are associated
with the purchase. This can include stamp duty (refer to the
section 'Don't forget stamp duty' earlier in this chapter), your
legal costs, settlement fees and loan charges. These loans are
usually referred to as 110 per cent loans, even though they're
rarely more than about 106 per cent (which largely depends on
stamp duty rates in your state or territory).

Here's an example to show how this works. Say a husband and
wife bought their home five years ago, paying $400,000 for the
house, and, because the home was their first, they took out a

loan of $350,000. Over the five years, the house grew in value to $540,000 — a rise of 35 per cent over the period. At the same time, they paid down the loan to $260,000.

When they do their sums and realise that their $50,000 equity has become $280,000 equity, they decide to buy an investment property. They find a place they like and believe they can get it for about $400,000. With a bit of help, they determine that the extra unavoidable costs on this property are going to be around $24,000, and they want to borrow the entire amount. When the bank sits down to look at their finance request, it follows an equation similar to this:

Current position:

House value: $540,000

House loan: $260,000

Loan-to-value ratio (LVR): 48.1 per cent

Investment loan request:

Investment property value: $400,000

Investment property loan: $424,000

Loan-to-value ratio (LVR): 106 per cent

Combined position after investment property purchase:

Value of joint properties: $940,000

Value of joint loans: $684,000

Combined loan-to-value ratio (LVR): 72.8 per cent

In total, even after the investment property's purchase, the net equity over the value of both properties has fallen slightly from $280,000 to $256,000. (The fall in equity is due to the stamp duty cost that has been borrowed, which has no equity value.)

Watch those bank valuations

When using equity in your home loan to borrow more money for investment, it's important to keep an eye on the valuation that the bank puts on your home when it's assessing your lending eligibility.

When a borrower applies for a new property loan, one of the bank's duties is to value the borrower's current assets. Usually, most banks pay a valuation company to conduct a *kerbside valuation*. This is almost as literal as it sounds. The valuer gets the official description of the house from government authorities, has a look at what properties have recently sold for in the area and then drives by the house. From the kerb, the valuer makes a few judgements on the value of the property.

Although most banks will share valuation details with you, not all banks do. You need to follow up with a request to find out the figure your property (or properties) is valued at.

 If you don't believe the valuation, query it. If you have proof that it's worth more — perhaps the bank and valuer are relying on out-of-date data — show the bank proof of recent sales. Sometimes it is worth asking for another valuation, this time insisting on an inspection of the inside of the house and the backyard. This can be especially important if the front of your house hasn't received as much love and attention as the inside and back. Bruce has regularly had valuations raised following internal inspections by a valuer.

Be aware, also, that valuers and valuation companies tend to be conservative by nature. They have to provide figures that hold up to their employer's scrutiny. They generally need to provide a figure that they believe it would sell for, if a quick sale were required. Not a fire-sale figure, but a price they believe the property would achieve if the market were to slow somewhat from its current point.

No Home? No Worries!

Property investors don't need to own their own home before launching into buying their first investment property. Far from it — buying an investment property is often a cheaper way to get into the property market than buying your own home. After all, you have a tenant who can help pay the mortgage.

After getting fired up about property investment from reading a personal finance book, Bruce decided that he wanted to buy a home to live in. After a discussion with Genevieve, now his wife, he was persuaded not to buy a 'home' and instead decided to buy an investment property.

Bruce bought the property, a detached unit in a block of three, in Heidelberg West in Melbourne, near the old village for the 1956 Melbourne Olympic Games. The unit cost $141,000. By the time Bruce and Genevieve had saved enough money between them to buy a home, the Heidelberg West property had appreciated and was worth $170,000. This is a strategy increasingly being used by younger people still living at home with their parents. They're often paying a peppercorn rent to their parents and have managed to save enough money for a house deposit. Someone may want to do this for many reasons, including not yet wanting the responsibilities that come with living in a home, wanting a foothold in the market or wanting to buy a place that they can move into later.

Advanced Funding Strategies

Sophisticated investors who develop an extensive real estate investment portfolio can employ a range of strategies to source capital. In the following sections, we outline those strategies, along with our advice for how to make them work.

Leveraging existing real estate investments

Over time, if the initial properties that you buy do what they're supposed to do, they'll appreciate in value. Thus, you may be able to use the equity from your successful investments as security to make more purchases, or *duplicate* your real estate investments. As we discuss in the section 'Borrowing Against Home Equity', earlier in this chapter, many investors begin by using equity in their owner-occupied home to fund other real estate purchases. By the same token, as you acquire more properties and they then appreciate, you can tap their equity for other purchases (see also Chapter 9 for information on how to build your investment portfolio).

As you build a real estate empire, you must be careful with exactly how much debt you take on. Property can go through long downturns and in some situations you could find yourself with vacant properties and falling rents. Excessively leveraged real estate investors can end up bankrupt.

Partners and investors

To accomplish larger deals, you may need or want to invest with a partner or other investors for the sake of diversification and risk reduction. Bringing in a partner can also provide additional financial resources for deposits and capital improvements, as well as greater borrowing capability.

Partners can be the best thing or the worst thing that ever happened to you. Although the additional financial resources may be essential when you're starting out in real estate, attempt to find partners with complementary skills to really take advantage of the potential of investment partnerships.

With the assistance of a good lawyer, prepare a legal contract to specify (among other issues) what happens if a partner wants out. A *buy/sell agreement* makes a lot of sense, because it outlines the terms and conditions in advance for how partnership assets can be redistributed. With life events (death, divorces, new marriages) constantly changing partnerships, having a buy/sell agreement in place at the time the partnership is established helps to prevent bickering down the road. Partnership disputes often only enrich lawyers and accountants.

Family members sometimes make good partners, but some families aren't suited to partnering to buy and operate real estate. Disputes over management style, cash distributions versus reinvesting in the property, and how and when to sell are difficult in any partnership but particularly in families where members may have different goals based on their age or personal desires. To minimise the potential problems, we strongly suggest documenting any real estate investment or lending relationship in writing just as diligently as you would with a non-family member.

Chapter 4

Financing Your Property Purchases

- -

- -

*Y*ou can't play if you can't pay. We know property investors who spent dozens to hundreds of hours finding the best locations and properties only to have their deals unravel when they were unable to gain approval for needed financing.

You probably also have questions about how to select the mortgage that's most appropriate for the property you're buying and your overall financial situation. This chapter covers the financing options you should consider (and some to avoid). In Chapter 5, we cover the actual process of applying for and locking up the specific loan you want.

Taking a Look at Mortgages

Although you can find thousands of different types of mortgages (thanks to all the various bells and whistles available), you need to understand the four basic mortgage types, covered in two groups. The first group focuses on the type of interest rates you can choose — *variable interest rates* or *fixed interest rates*. The second group involves a decision on whether your repayments will be *interest-only* or also repay part of the

borrowed capital, called a *principal and interest (P&I) loan*.
All mortgages combine at least one element from the first group
with one from the second group. But mortgages can combine
both elements of each group — interest rates can be fixed for
a number of years and then have a variable interest rate after
that, and the repayments can start off as interest-only and then
later switch to principal and interest. In the following sections,
we discuss these major loan types, what features they typically
have and how you can intelligently compare them with each
other and select the one that best fits with your investment
property purchases.

Going with the flow: Variable-rate mortgages

The vast majority of mortgages taken out in Australia — whether
to buy investment properties or homes — are taken out as
variable-rate mortgages, usually for terms of 25 or 30 years.
Variable-rate mortgages carry an interest rate that changes over
time, roughly tracking the changes made by the Reserve Bank
of Australia (RBA) to the 'official cash rate'. Prior to the GFC,
whatever change the RBA made to the cash rate was matched
equally by the major lenders. However, lenders' 'costs of
financing' changed dramatically following the GFC and banks no
longer move in lock step with the RBA. The RBA can make, say,
a cut of 0.5 percentage points, but the banks may then only pass
on 0.3 or 0.4 percentage points. And when the RBA has increased
rates by, say, 0.25 percentage points, the banks have actually
increased their rates by 0.3 or 0.4 percentage points. In 2013 at
the time of writing, this situation is slowly sorting itself out, as
volatility in global capital markets subsides.

A variable-rate mortgage starts with a set interest rate, but can
move up or down each and every month. In practice, variable
rates tend to move only a few times each year. Because a
variable interest rate changes over time, so too does the size of
the loan's monthly repayment. Variable rates are attractive for a
number of reasons:

 ✔ At most points of the interest rates cycle, variable rates are
    lower than fixed rates. So, given the economics of a typical
    investment property purchase, variable rates are more
    likely to enable you to achieve positive cash flow in the
    early years of property ownership.

> ✔ Should interest rates decline, you can realise most, if not
> all, of the benefits of lower rates without the cost and
> hassle of refinancing. With a fixed-rate mortgage (which we
> discuss later in this chapter), the only way to benefit from
> an overall decline in the market level of interest rates is to
> refinance, which can result in expensive exit fees from your
> current loan.

Depending on the individual lender's policies, variable-rate loans
usually come with many more features and options than do
fixed-rate mortgages. But variable rates also come in two broad
types — standard and discount variable rates.

Standard variable rates

The *standard variable rate* (SVR) is generally a lender's full-
service loan product. Although it has a different name at
almost every banking institution, SVR is the figure most often
quoted by the media when they talk about mortgage interest
rates, or rising or falling interest rates. The SVR is usually
the highest rate charged to general mortgage customers, but
often comes with other products — which can be useful to
some customers — thrown in, such as offset accounts, redraw
accounts and fee-free general banking (see Chapter 5 for more
information on these products).

But, despite the fact that the SVR is the most often quoted
interest rate, few customers actually pay it. Customers —
particularly property investors, who tend to have higher average
total loan balances — find that most banks discount the offered
interest rate from the SVR.

Discount variable rates

The 'no-frills' mortgage product, *discount variable rates*,
is usually advertised at 0.4 to 0.9 per cent lower than a
standard variable rate. However, these rates won't always offer
access to products such as offset accounts, redraw accounts
and fee-free banking.

These lower rate products may suit you when you're starting
out with your first, relatively low-value, investment property.
However, even if you're buying a more expensive first investment
property, a bank, if asked, will offer all the extras available
with a standard variable rate, but at an interest rate normally
associated with a discounted loan (see Chapter 5 for more
information on banking products).

Honeymoon rates

Lenders often offer an introductory rate for a mortgage, known as a *honeymoon rate*. Don't be fooled though: You won't pay this tantalisingly low rate for very long. These rates are inevitably offered for periods of as short as four or five months, or as long as a year. This rate is referred to as a honeymoon rate because the lower initial interest rate gives the borrower a gentle easing-in to the longer term costs of a mortgage. The introductory rate is often set artificially low to entice you into the product. In other words, even if the market level of interest rates doesn't change, your variable-rate mortgage is destined to increase at the end of the defined honeymoon period. An increase of one or two percentage points is common.

Annualised average percentage rates

Much more important than an artificially low introductory interest rate is the average cost of the loan over a given period — that is, if the rate is cheaper at the start and more expensive later, what's the average cost over, say, seven years?

This concern over borrowers being seduced or duped by low introductory rates led to the introduction of *annualised average percentage rates* (AAPRs) to interest-rate advertising by Australian lenders. The AAPR, also sometimes referred to as a *comparison rate* or a *true rate*, is designed to force lenders to bundle all of the associated costs of a loan — such as interest rates, fees and charges — and average them over a seven-year period for the purpose of advertising the 'true' cost of the mortgage. AAPRs make it easier for customers to compare rates offered by various lenders and to realise that a honeymoon rate might not be such a great deal.

What does this mean for potential borrowers? It means you'll often see an interest rate advertised for a product with a different rate alongside it, often in a different size, colour or typeface, or with an asterisk nearby. Almost inevitably, the lower rate is the loan's advertised interest rate. The higher figure is likely to be the AAPR, or the one that takes in all costs and fees over a seven-year period. It's not uncommon for a honeymoon rate (refer to the preceding section) of 6.5 per cent, for example, to have an AAPR of 8 per cent. That is, the average cost of the loan over seven years will be 8 per cent. By comparison, another loan advertised as having a rate of 7.3 per cent may have an AAPR of just 7.6 per cent, making it a 'cheaper' loan.

But low comparison rates aren't the most important factor in determining which loan is best for you. Loans may have low AAPRs because they don't have some other loan functions that you may want, or need (see Chapter 5 for other loan features that investors may wish to consider as part of their mortgage funding requirements).

The security of fixed-rate mortgages

Considerably less common than variable-rate mortgages in Australia, *fixed-rate mortgages* tend to be offered for periods of between one and ten years, depending on the individual lender. The interest rate remains constant over the life of the agreed loan term. Because the interest rate stays the same, your monthly mortgage payment stays the same.

For the purpose of making future estimates of your property's cash flow, fixed-rate mortgages can offer you certainty and some peace of mind, because you know precisely your mortgage payment for a fixed period. (Of course, the property's other costs — such as property taxes, insurance and maintenance — will still escalate over the years.)

Peace of mind has a price, though. The following points examine some of the conditions of fixed-rate mortgages:

- ✔ Fixed-rate loans are usually inflexible. Many lenders won't let you make extra repayments or, if they do, only under restricted conditions. Should you need to sell your property, you might find that you're locked into repayments for the fixed period, or face hefty exit fees.

- ✔ Depending on the stage of the credit cycle, fixed rates normally incur an interest rate premium compared with variable rate loans. In other words, you're paying a premium for your 'peace of mind'.

- ✔ If, like most investment property buyers, you're facing a tough time generating a healthy positive cash flow in the early years of owning a particular investment property, a fixed-rate mortgage may make it even more financially challenging. A variable-rate mortgage, by contrast, can lower your property's carrying costs in those early years. (Refer to the section 'Going with the flow: Variable-rate mortgages' earlier in this chapter.)

- ✔ Fixed-rate loans carry the risk of being locked into higher interest rates when variable rates are falling.

While fixed rates can increase your property's carrying costs, they can be invaluable if the interest rates are locked in at a low point of the interest rate cycle. If, for example, you've locked in a rate of 6 per cent and then interest rates rise, say, 2 per cent, you have a very cheap source of financing until your locked-in period finishes.

Tax-effective interest-only loans

Many Australians have been brought up with a fear of debt. From the time many of us start to learn about money, it's rammed into our heads that when you get a loan (for any purpose), your primary goal is to get that loan repaid as quickly as possible. In the extreme, some people believe you should put your enjoyment of life itself on hold until the loan is repaid. But buying property — be it a home or an investment — almost inevitably requires borrowed money. And, although it may shock some to hear this, it often makes financial sense to never pay the bank their money back! Just pay interest — that is, rent the bank's money — forever.

Australia's tax laws at the time of writing state that interest paid on money borrowed to fund income-producing investments is tax-deductible, whereas repayment of investment capital and personal, non-investment debt is not deductible. So, if you have an *interest-only* loan on an investment property, in most cases, all of your interest costs qualify as a tax deduction. However, repaying the original borrowings does not qualify as a deduction. All repayment of money for personal loans (including your home, cars, holidays and credit cards) is also generally not tax-deductible.

Whether the loan interest is tax-deductible or not is the basis of what is often referred to as the *good debt/bad debt* principle. If you have a number of loans, some of which are investment (good debt) and some of which are personal (bad debt), you should always aim to pay off the bad debt before attacking repayment of any of the good debt. The only exception may be if the interest rate on the good debt was *significantly* higher than the rate on your bad debt (which is rarely, if ever, the case with investment property).

Here's an example of the good debt/bad debt principle: Assume an investment property loan of $380,000, with an interest rate of 7.5 per cent. If the loan is interest-only, the repayments required each year will be $28,500. Under most circumstances (assuming that the property is rented or available for rent) and with most investment properties, that entire $28,500 will be a tax deduction. However, if the same loan is a 25-year principal and interest (P&I) loan, the annual repayment in the first year will be about $33,697. Of that sum, $28,317 will be interest and $5,380 will be repayment of principal and won't be deductible. Only the $28,317 will be a tax deduction. Although little difference exists between the two sums that qualify as a deduction, the investor still has to find $5,380 extra each year for repayment of principal that he won't have to find on an interest-only loan.

'But at least the loan is being repaid!' is the reaction of many. If this is the only loan that an investor has, repaying principal might be preferable. And nothing is wrong with repaying loan principal. However, it's not always the most tax-effective solution for an investor. In particular, if investors who have other non-deductible debt accelerate payments on their personal debt, they're usually better off in two ways. Most investors have some money owing on their own home. By focusing repayment of principal onto the home loan, the investor is both minimising the non-deductible interest on the home loan and maximising tax-deductible interest payments on the investment loan.

To take the previous example one step further, if the investor uses that $5,380 to pay down his own home loan, he'll save himself about $403 in interest on the home loan (which would compound the following year).

Many lenders only insist on principal being repaid from one of their loans. If you have a home loan and an investment property loan (or many investment property loans) with the same lender, the lender may want you to repay principal on the home loan, but allow long-term, interest-only repayments on the remainder.

The downside of interest-only loans is that the amount of money owed against the property doesn't fall. If you buy a property with a $400,000 loan, after three years of interest-only repayments, you'll still owe the bank $400,000.

Making a dent with principal and interest loans

For a principal and interest (P&I) loan, the borrower agrees to pay the lender not only the interest on the loan, but also some of the initial capital each week, month or year. Over the term of the loan, which is usually 25 or 30 years for mortgages in Australia, the initial sum borrowed is repaid in full and the mortgage comes to an end.

Apart from the effect of changes to official interest rates, P&I loan repayments are constant throughout the term of the loan. What changes during that period is the amount of money that's assigned as interest and the amount that's designated as repayment of capital. The reduction in the principal component of the loan is worked out by a mathematical formula known as *amortisation*. Initially, the majority of the repayment is designated as interest repayments and a small amount is to repay the initial capital, or principal. And as the principal gets paid down, the amount of interest reduces and the amount used to pay off principal increases.

Here's an example: A 25-year, $420,000 principal and interest loan with a 7.5 per cent interest rate will require repayments of $3,103.76 a month. In the first month of repayment, $2,625 will go towards interest and $478.76 will be repayment of principal. At the end of the first year, the amount being directed to interest versus principal repayment won't have changed very much — $2,591.04 will be interest and $512.72 will go towards principal. However, at the end of the 12th year, the $3,103.76 will be split as $1,867.61 for interest and $1,125.30 for principal. The final repayment, when the loan is finally paid out, will be $18.59 in interest and $2,974.32 as the last principal repayment.

An owner has two ways to increase the amount of equity in a property (refer to Chapter 3 for a discussion of home equity). The first is that the value of the property itself increases; the second is that the value of the loan decreases. P&I loans are one option investors can exercise control over in increasing their equity ownership in a property.

Making Some Decisions

You can't (or at least shouldn't) spend months deciding which mortgage may be right for your situation. So, in the following sections, we help you zero in on mortgages suitable for you.

Deciding between variable and fixed

Choosing between a variable-rate and a fixed-rate loan is an important decision in the real estate investment process. Consider the advantages and disadvantages of each mortgage type and decide what's best for your situation prior to refinancing or purchasing real estate.

How much risk can you handle in regard to the size of your property's monthly mortgage payment? If you can take the financial risks that come with a variable rate — the main risk being that your mortgage could rise considerably if the Reserve Bank, or your bank, raises interest rates — you have a better chance of maximising your property's cash flow with a variable-rate rather than a fixed-rate loan. Variable interest rates tend to remain lower over the course of an economic cycle. Even if rates go up, they'll likely come back down over the life of your loan. If you always stick with variable loans, you will usually come out ahead.

If your income (and applicable investment property cash flow) significantly exceeds your spending, you may feel less anxiety about a fluctuating variable interest rate. If you do choose a variable loan, you may feel more secure if you have a sizeable financial cushion of a few months' expenses reserved, which you can access if rates go up.

Some people take variable rates without thoroughly understanding whether they can really afford them. When rates rise, property owners who can't afford higher payments face a financial crisis. If you don't have emergency savings you can tap into to make the higher payments, how can you afford the monthly payments and the other expenses of your property? Bank loan approval processes generally build in a buffer when trying to determine whether a borrower can afford to meet higher repayments, in case interest rates rise. If interest rates at the time of an application were 7 per cent, the bank would want to be satisfied that the customer could meet repayments if interest rates were to rise to 9 or 10 per cent. The banks' system is obviously not foolproof, and smaller or less scrupulous lenders may not be as diligent in assessing a customer's repayment power before approving a loan.

Some property experts recommend locking in for a long time when rates are cheap, whereas others believe it's best to fix rates for only short periods when you believe the market has temporarily mispriced likely future interest rate movements.

Fixed interest rates tend to reflect the level that professional investors believe rates are heading towards over the fixed rate term. If investors believe interest rates are likely to fall over the next couple of years, one- and two-year fixed rates may be lower than some variable interest rates. If they believe that interest rates are heading up, fixed rates may be higher than variable rates. You also can have short- and long-term fixed rates on different sides of current variable rates. If investors believe the Reserve Bank is likely to cut interest rates over the short term (possibly to add extra stimulus to the economy) but raise them in the medium to long term, short-term fixed rates may be below current variable rates, while longer-term rates may be above. This scenario can also work in the reverse.

You may also consider a split loan — fixing a portion, but leaving the remainder at variable rates. If rates do rise, only half your mortgage will require higher repayments. The opposite applies if rates fall.

Deciding between interest-only and principal and interest

The decision on whether to take an interest-only or principal and interest (P&I) loan should be a simple one. If you have other non-deductible, or 'bad', debt (such as a home, car or personal loan), it makes more sense to have an interest-only loan for your investment property. Any savings should be redirected to repaying the principal on loans that can't be claimed as a tax deduction, particularly your home (refer to the section 'Tax-effective interest-only loans' earlier in this chapter).

Some investors — young people buying an investment property before buying their first home and older people who've paid off their home — won't have any bad debt and may want to repay the principal on their investment loan as a way of building equity faster.

Deciding on a loan term

Most mortgage lenders offer you the option of 25-year or 30-year mortgages. Borrowers can also ask for shorter loan terms. So, how do you decide whether a shorter or longer term mortgage is best for your investment property purchase?

The difference in repayments between 25- and 30-year loan terms isn't significant. On a $400,000 loan at 7.5 per cent, a 25-year term would have P&I monthly repayments of $2,956, whereas a 30-year term would have $2,797. This decision is often a function of whether you choose to pay interest-only or P&I. If you choose P&I because you'd rather repay your debt faster, you may also want a shorter term.

 If you decide on a 30-year mortgage over a 25-year mortgage, or a 25-year mortgage over a 20-year mortgage, you may still maintain the flexibility to pay the mortgage off faster if you choose to.

Reviewing Other Common Lending Fees

Whether the loan is variable or fixed, mortgage lenders typically levy other up-front fees and charges. These ancillary fees can really amount to quite a bundle with some lenders. Here's our take on the typical extra charges you're likely to encounter — including what's reasonable and what's not:

✔ **Application fee:** Most lenders charge $300 to $1,500 to process your paperwork and see it through their loan-evaluation process. If your loan's rejected, or if it's approved and you decide not to take it, the lender *usually* won't charge this fee. If you're applying for a loan through a mortgage broker and the loan is successful, the fee may be part of the broker's remuneration.

✔ **Valuation fee:** The property you're borrowing money to buy needs to be valued. If you default on your mortgage, a lender doesn't want to be stuck with a property that's worth less than you owe. The cost for valuation ranges from $0 to $800 for typical purchases. More banks are picking up the tab for this expense in the hope of luring customers.

✔ **Legal fee:** About half of Australia's lenders charge a fee to cover their legal costs of *conveyancing* (the legal transfer of property), a fee that can be a nominal fee of $50 to $150, or run up to $500.

✔ **Settlement fee:** Many lenders charge a fee to attend to the actual process of *settlement* — the final signatures that transfer the ownership of the property and finalise mortgage documents for the new owner.

Request a detailed list of other fees and charges in writing from all lenders you're seriously considering. You need to know the total of all lender fees so you can accurately compare different lenders' loans and determine how much settling on your loan is going to cost you.

 Most banks or mortgage brokers will run your application through a pre-approval process for free, which usually gives you a fairly clear indication of whether the bank is going to lend you the money and how much they'll lend you. If this process indicates that you'll be approved for a loan, you can ask for the pre-approval in writing, which will allow you to bid or negotiate more confidently for a property.

Alternatively, to reduce the possibility of wasting your time and money applying for a mortgage you may not qualify for, disclose up-front any credit issues you have and ask the lender if your situation suggests any reasons you may not be approved. By raising your credit issues and explaining them, you may find that the lender is willing to look around the issue or that their processes are too inflexible to do so. Either way, it may be better than going through the entire process, only to be knocked back.

Mortgages That Should Make You Think Twice

As well as the more standard loans (refer to the section 'Taking a Look at Mortgages' earlier in this chapter), you may come across other loans such as interest-capitalising loans and recourse loans (where a lender can come after your own home if you fail to meet repayments on your investment property). Here, we present our thoughts on the risks associated with these loans.

Interest-capitalising loans

With an interest-capitalising loan, the investor doesn't pay the interest and the interest itself is *capitalised* onto the loan. Although this loan, in theory, is even more tax-effective than an interest-only loan, we consider these loans as taking one risk too many.

When you add interest to a loan, you add a compounding impact, just like interest paid on a savings account. In the

first year of capitalising your interest on a $300,000 loan
(at 7.5 per cent), your loan grows to more than $323,000. In the
second year, the loan balance grows to more than $348,000. By
the end of the tenth year, the loan will be more than $613,600.
This means that, if you sold the house after ten years, its value
would need to have increased by 7.5 per cent a year, compound,
just to repay the loan.

The Tax Office is constantly monitoring these sorts of loans
and has occasionally challenged them in the courts and won.
Borrowers entering into these sorts of loans should be wary of
the potential that an adverse ATO ruling could have on their
personal finances. They are best steered clear of.

Recourse financing

Among the many factors to explore before agreeing to any loan,
you also want to consider whether the loan is non-recourse
or recourse, or even limited recourse (for self-managed super
funds):

- ✔ **Non-recourse loans:** In the event that you fail to fulfil the
  terms of your loan, this type of loan limits the lender to
  foreclosing only on the property financed by the loan.
  Foreclosure is the full and complete satisfaction of the loan,
  and the lender can't seek a deficiency judgement or go
  after your other assets, such as your home. These types of
  loans are rare in Australia for property loans.

- ✔ **Recourse loans:** These loans lower the lender's risk
  because they offer additional protection. If the terms of
  your loan aren't fulfilled, the lender has the legal right to
  go after your other assets to cover any shortfall, should
  the property value not fully cover the outstanding debt
  balance. Remember that, after a loan is in default, the
  interest penalties and legal fees can add up quickly.
  If you're already in default on the loan for your rental
  property, you may not want a lender taking your home or
  other viable rental properties to satisfy the shortfall. Full
  recourse loans are the most common type of loan offered
  for personal property loans.

- ✔ **Limited-recourse loans:** These loans are a legal
  requirement of loans to self-managed super funds (SMSFs).

Lenders prefer recourse financing. If you're prepared to put up
other properties (including your home) as security, a lender

feels more secure. If you don't want to put up other homes as surety (non-recourse), you may have to pay a higher interest rate or put up more of a deposit for the property.

As long as you're not too aggressive and don't over-leverage your rental properties, real estate investing can be relatively safe, and the chances are you won't be faced with losing other properties by defaulting on your loan. But you are limited in your ability to control all the diverse economic factors that can affect your property.

Vendor's Terms

A common way of selling property a century or so ago, when banks were only for the rich, was to effectively borrow the money from the vendor, to be repaid over an agreed term. *Vendor's terms* is a transaction in which the seller (the vendor) accepts terms other than all cash at closing, such as borrowing the remaining funds from the vendor and repaying her as you might a regular mortgage, or offering partial settlement through swapping another asset (property, business interest or a vehicle).

Not every seller needs or even wants to receive all cash up-front as payment for a property, so you may be able to finance part or even all of an investment property purchase under vendor's terms with the property seller's financing. This is a rare way to buy a property in Australia, but it is possible.

The best candidates for vendor's terms are vendors with significant equity or those who own the property outright.

Occasionally sellers will offer this option but, in other cases, you need to pop the question. We can think of two good reasons to ask for the seller to help finance an investment property purchase:

 ✔ **Better terms:** Mortgage lenders, typically banks or large monolithic financial institutions, aren't particularly flexible businesses. You may well be able to obtain a lower interest rate, lower or waived fees, and more flexible repayment conditions from a property seller. Conventional loans also carry many expenses that a property seller may not require, including loan-application fees, account-keeping fees and a valuation.

✔ **Loan approval:** Perhaps you've had prior financial problems that have caused mortgage lenders to routinely deny your mortgage applications. Some property sellers may be more flexible, especially in a slow real estate market or with a property that's challenging to sell. A seller can also make a decision in a few days, whereas a conventional lender may take weeks.

Be careful when considering a property if a seller is offering financing as part of the deal. This factor may be a sign of a hard-to-sell property. Investigate how long the property has been on the market and what specific flaws and problems it may have.

Some of the reasons sellers may offer their own financing are

✔ **They're attracted to the potential returns of being a mortgage lender.** This reason shouldn't concern the buyer as long as the terms of the seller financing are reasonable.

✔ **They're seeking a price that exceeds the normal conventional loan parameters, or the property doesn't qualify for a conventional loan for some reason.** Examples of qualification issues include a cracked slab and environmental issues. This is a risky scenario for buyers and may be an indication that they're over-reaching or pursuing a property that's not a good investment.

When financing on vendor's terms, make sure that the agreement is non-recourse (refer to the section 'Recourse financing' earlier in this chapter) and watch out for a due-on-sale clause. A *due-on-sale* clause is a requirement that stipulates that, if you sell the house while you still owe the original vendor money, your first obligation is to pay the original vendor out the remaining owed funds (meaning you can't effectively take the loan and transfer it to your next property). This clause is fine in an agreement, but you need to be aware of it, because it may affect your future financing options.

Chapter 5

Shopping for and Securing the Best Mortgage Terms

*I*n Chapter 4, we consider the differences between the many loan options available so you can select the one that best suits your personal and financial situation. If you've started delving into the different types of real estate investment financing, you may have already begun the process of speaking with different lenders and surfing internet sites.

In this chapter, we provide our top tips and advice for shopping for and ultimately securing the best financing that you can for your real estate investment purchases and refinances. We also cover how to attribute rental income and deal with common loan problems that may derail your plans.

Shopping for Mortgages

Mortgage costs of your real estate investment purchases are generally the single biggest ongoing expense by far, so it pays to shop around and know how to unearth the best deals. You're likely to find that many lenders would love to have your business, especially if you have a strong credit rating. Although having numerous lenders competing for your business can save you money, it can also make mortgage shopping and selection difficult. The following sections should help you to simplify matters.

Putting your existing relationship to the test

In Australian society today, with so much money moving around through cyberspace via electronic transactions, virtually everybody needs a bank account. The most basic of all accounts is a savings account, but most people considering a property investment have hopefully tested a number of other products, including credit cards, a personal loan, a car loan, a cheque account and even a home loan. Having any sort of account means you have a relationship with a lender. And, if you believe you have a reasonable relationship with that lender, why not ask if you can extend the friendship?

As a first port of call, ask to speak to a loans manager at your local institution, whether that's a bank, building society or credit union. A general rule of business — but particularly in banking — is that it's far cheaper to keep a customer than to find a new one. Businesses hate losing good customers. And, if you have a good credit record, you may find that your bank wants to keep you.

But this is just a first step. If you're buying property for the first time, and particularly if it's your first time getting a loan, *don't* accept the first offer made to you by your own bank. Treat your first application as a practice interview, if you like, while you find the best source of financing for you.

Mulling over mortgage brokers

Mortgage brokers came to the fore in the early 1990s, when banks went through a cost-cutting period, which involved culling staff and shutting branches. The former branch and lending managers were among those to be sacked. But banks still needed to write loans, so mortgage brokers — usually ex-branch managers — began writing loans for lenders.

Mortgage brokers are recommended for novice property investors. For a start, they have access to a wide range of banks on their books, potentially saving you a lot of time in trying to compare products. They should also be able to answer all of your questions about the various products that you may, or may not, want to consider as part of your funding package (although we cover much of what you need to know about the important products later in this chapter).

Look for mortgage brokers who have at least a dozen lenders on their books, but preferably 30 or 40. Brokers are paid in one of two ways. The vast majority are paid by the banks via an up-front fee and a trailing commission. Some brokers charge a *fee-for-service,* a flat fee paid by the borrower, where commissions paid to the broker are rebated to the customer or the loan interest rate itself is discounted.

 As with all sales industries, the finance industry continues to debate whether commissions affect the quality of advice given. The argument goes that a fee-for-service broker is likely to recommend the best product for the customer because he gets paid the same amount of money no matter what product he recommends. One concern is whether a commission-based broker is likely to recommend a product that doesn't pay her a commission. Or, perhaps, whether she is less likely to recommend a product from a bank that pays her significantly less commission than another bank's product. Usually, a commission-based broker is a cheaper up-front option for the customer. In effect, the customer pays nothing, because the bank pays the fees to the broker. The bank also pays a trailing fee, which continues for the life of the loan, to the broker. A *trailing fee* is essentially paid in recognition that the broker will continue to provide service to the customer. A fee-for-service broker tends to cost more up-front, but he may be able to arrange a better long-term deal for the customer. Neither a fee-for-service nor a commission broker is a guarantee that you're going to get the best product.

Keeping up with commissions

A mortgage broker is typically paid a percentage, usually between 0.5 and 0.65 per cent, of the loan amount. In most circumstances, a trailing commission is also paid to the adviser, in the vicinity of 0.15 per cent. This commission is negotiable, especially on larger loans, which are more lucrative. (The commissions on larger deals, in some cases, are capped at a dollar figure by the lender.)

Be sure to ask what the commission is on every alternative loan that a broker pitches. Some brokers may get indignant — that's their problem. You have every right to ask; after all, it's your right to make a decision as to whether a broker's pushing you in the direction of a higher commission payment.

Even if you plan to shop on your own, talking to a mortgage broker may be worthwhile. At the very least, you can compare what you find with what brokers say they can get for you. Again, be careful. Some brokers tell you what you want to hear — that is, that they can beat your best find — and then aren't able to deliver when the time comes.

Counting a broker's contributions

A good mortgage broker can make the following contributions to your real estate investing team:

- ✔ **Advice:** If you're like most people, you may have a difficult time deciding which type of mortgage is best for your situation. A good mortgage broker can take the time to listen to your financial and personal situation and goals, and offer suggestions for specific loans that match.

- ✔ **Shopping:** Even after you figure out the specific type of mortgage you want, dozens of lenders may offer that type of loan. (You'll find fewer lender options for commercial properties.)

  A good mortgage broker can probably save you time and money by shopping for the best deal. Brokers can be especially helpful if you have a less-than-pristine credit report or you want to buy property with a low deposit — 10 per cent or less of the value of a property. (Purchasing commercial, industrial or retail property with less than a 20 to 30 per cent deposit or equity is quite difficult.)

- ✔ **Paperwork and presentation:** An organised and detail-oriented mortgage broker can assist you with completing the morass of forms most lenders demand. Mortgage brokers can assist you with preparing your loan package so that you put your best foot forward with lenders.

  The larger the loan, the more involved and complicated the paperwork. Have your personal financial statement prepared in advance so it can be easily updated, because, each time you seek a loan for an investment property, you're required to provide a current financial statement to the broker (and all potential loan sources).

✔ **Closing the deal:** After you sign a contract, you still have much to do before settlement. A competent mortgage broker can make sure you meet the important settlement deadlines.

Looking for loans on the internet

There's little that can't be found on the internet, certainly when it comes to information. And, when you come to research the right loan product, an hour or two surfing the Net can be invaluable.

In our experience, the internet is better used for mortgage research than for securing a specific mortgage. That's not to say that some sites can't provide competitive loans in a timely fashion. However, we've seen some property purchases fall apart because the buyers relied upon a website that failed to deliver a loan in time.

Here's a shortlist of some of our favourite mortgage-related internet sites you may find helpful:

✔ **Ratings agencies:** The two most established sites that allow you to compare products with little bias are Infochoice (www.infochoice.com.au) and Canstar (www.cannex.com.au), which have both developed strong reputations as independent information providers. But be wary of only accepting *sponsored* links through these websites — these are links to those lenders who pay extra for promotion. The sites also provide direct links to bank websites, and can help with information on the various state government fees that are charged on property transactions.

✔ **Australian Bankers' Association:** The once-tainted ABA (www.bankers.asn.au) has worked hard to regain the respect of Australian consumers and has built a sizeable site of useful information for those who use banking products.

✔ **Government-related sites:** The websites of the Reserve Bank of Australia (www.rba.gov.au) and the Australian Bureau of Statistics (www.abs.gov.au) contain an incredible array of economic data. The facts and figures contained therein are the sort of information that the RBA uses to determine interest-rate policy.

✔ **Bank sites:** Major lenders now have no shortage of information on their websites. Once you have narrowed down your search to a few lenders, you might want to try their sites.

✔ **Mortgage brokers:** Dozens of large and small mortgage brokers out there are fighting for your business. Simply punch in 'mortgage broker' to a search engine and you will find no shortage of them, many of which have websites with useful information and calculators.

Relying on referrals

Some sources of real estate advice simply tell you to get referrals in your quest to find the best mortgage lenders. Sounds simple and straightforward — but it's not. For example, loans for commercial investment properties have different lender-underwriting requirements and terms compared with residential loans.

Good referrals can be a useful tool for locating the best lenders. Here are a few sources we recommend:

✔ Start with a bank or credit union you currently have a relationship with and then seek referrals from them if they're not interested in making the specific loan you have in mind.

✔ Collect referrals from people who you know and trust and who've demonstrated some ability to select good service providers. Start with the best professional service providers (tax advisers, lawyers, financial advisers, real estate agents and so on) you know and respect, and ask them for their recommendations.

Don't take anyone's referrals as gospel. Always be wary of businesspeople who refer you to business contacts or colleagues who have referred business to them over the years. Whenever you get a recommendation, ask the people doing the referring why they're making the referral and what they like and don't like about the service provider. And ask if any money changes hands between the two businesses — that can be an indication of the motivation of the referrer.

Economies of Scale

Most consumers understand the concept of economies of scale, even if they don't understand the actual meaning of the term as used by economists. In economic terms, *economies of scale* are where the cost of a unit decreases because large quantities of the item are being produced or bought. A simpler version for consumers is: When you walk into a supermarket, a single can of soft drink may cost you $1. But if you buy a box of 30 cans of soft drink, the box may cost you $15, or 50 cents per can. Buying banking products is no different.

Buying banking in bulk

Lenders are prepared to offer you discounts if you purchase enough banking products through them. How much extra work is needed to look after you if you have both a home loan and an investment mortgage with a bank? Twice as much? Probably not. What happens if you have a home loan, two investment property mortgages, a credit card and a car loan? The bank is making a margin on a bunch of products. In this situation, a competitor might cut its margins slightly in order to win your business. So, to keep your custom, a smart lender will keep you satisfied with special discounts. The concept is no different from any other aspect of business — bigger customers get better rates.

In fact, most banks now offer volume discounts even if you have a single loan product. Home mortgage loans of more than $150,000 often incur a discount to the standard home loan rate, and those with more than $250,000 may get a higher discount. Still-larger discounts may be offered to those with more than $500,000 or $700,000 worth of home loans (see the section 'Considering a Professional Package' later in this chapter).

Property investors obviously tend to have larger-than-average loan volumes. They often have a home mortgage and also need a mortgage on their investment property. If you buy a second or a third investment property, you can quickly find yourself with more than $1 million of debt. And, for a bank, that's an attractive amount of money to be charging interest on.

Taking on bigger and bigger debt

To begin property investing you need to have a solid understanding of debt. And you need to be comfortable with large debt. Moving from having a mortgage on your home to having a mortgage on your home *and* an investment property often means a doubling of debt (but not a doubling of your net interest costs, thanks to the deductibility of interest on investment loans). Large investment property debt is covered in more detail in Chapter 9.

When you've been investing in property for a while, you may even accumulate multimillion-dollar debts on your property portfolio. Big debt scares a lot of people off property investment. But getting comfortable with larger debt is the best (and most tax-effective) way to build a portfolio of property assets.

Sizing Up Banking Products

Literally thousands of mortgage products and options are on offer, and hundreds of lenders, some of which offer dozens of combinations of loans each. How on earth are you supposed to find the perfect one for you? Relax. You probably won't find the perfect one. The best thing to do is make sure the loan you settle on suits you and your situation, and offers a level of service you find acceptable.

The starting point is to find out about the basic products and whether or not you need or want them.

Interest rates: Is cheaper always better?

The biggest ongoing cost of property investment is usually the interest being paid on the loan. That is almost certainly the case in the early stages of an investment if you use a loan to fund most of your purchase. So, putting in the groundwork to find a good relationship and a cheap source of funding makes sense.

The sharp increase in the number of lenders since the mid-1980s has meant a considerable increase in competition. Competition has been good for borrowers on two main fronts. The first is that competition squeezes interest rate margins — making loans considerably cheaper — and the second is that the variety of lending products has expanded dramatically.

The global financial crisis put an end to the interest rate squeeze suffered by banks, which had been so wonderful for consumers. Interest rate *margins* — the difference between the interest rate banks pay to get the money and the rate at which they lend it out — increased from early 2008 until early 2013. The foundation of the GFC was actually a global *credit* crisis and those lending the credit to banks to on-lend to borrowers started demanding two things. First, they wanted higher rates paid for their credit. Second, they wanted less risk. Both of those demands increased the cost of funding to the banks, which have passed the costs on in the form of higher interest rates to consumers. In early 2013 a discounting war broke out, signalling potentially better times for borrowers.

The cheapest source of funding isn't necessarily always the best. Usually, the cheaper the interest rate on a loan, the fewer bells and whistles attached. Nothing is wrong with hunting down the cheapest interest rate when you're sourcing an investment property, but another product with a slightly higher interest rate may save you money in the long run.

Most lenders can quote a range of interest rates, which often only serves to confuse potential customers. But, when it comes down to variable-rate mortgages, you'll find two main types — standard variable and discount variable. Standard variable rates (lenders may have different names for their own product) come with all the bells and whistles and, naturally, a higher interest rate. (But investors will get a discount on this rate.) Discount variable rates are usually 0.4 to 1.0 percentage points lower than the standard variable rate, but may not have some of the other products (discussed in the following sections) that you may, or may not, need. Refer to Chapter 4 for more on different basic mortgage types.

Merging your home and investment finances

Most people approaching their first investment property have already bought their own home and probably still have a home loan. Taking on extra investment debt can have advantages — you might find that banks are keener to keep you, or lure you, with lower interest rates or extra products that may be useful in your personal life, such as free credit cards, redraw and offset accounts or rewards programs.

Few banks offer particularly rewarding discounts if you have loans of less than $150,000. So the addition of an investment property mortgage — which will usually be more than $350,000 — may give you loans of more than $500,000. And that suddenly makes you considerably more appealing to a lender. Previously you may have been paying full price on a standard variable loan and the associated frills, or have been on a discount variable rate, without the benefits. With most banks, if you're about to sign up for an additional investment property mortgage, you only have to ask in order to get all the benefits of a standard variable loan for the price of a discount variable loan.

Don't be taken for granted

An investor couple Bruce knows managed to buy three investment properties within a few years, running up debt of more than $800,000. Each time the couple wanted a new property, they went back to the same lender and requested another loan. The couple owned their own home outright, had sufficient income to repay the loans, and were good customers.

For their first property, the bank started them off on the normal rate for a loan of that level, about $250,000. When they came back and borrowed another $260,000, the bank lent them the money at the same rate. And the same with the third property, which cost another $300,000 of debt.

They finally asked Bruce about their situation. He said that, with that much debt, most banks would, at that time, offer to beat their existing bank's interest rate by 0.6 per cent, purely because they had more than $800,000 worth of debt. Unfortunately, the original lender had steep exit fees. However, the couple bit the bullet, paid the exit fees and transferred to another lender. The interest savings effectively paid off the exit fees within 18 months and the couple was ahead by nearly $5,000 a year after that on their existing loans, but had further savings as their property portfolio expanded. Since then, the couple has received further discounts and now get a 0.9 per cent discount to the standard variable rate charged by the bank.

Here's an example of how increasing your debt can give your bank an incentive to lower your interest rate: You may have been paying a standard variable interest rate of 8 per cent for a $180,000 loan. But the addition of a $400,000 investment property loan gives you $580,000 of total business with the bank. You could rightly expect to see your interest rate cut by up to 0.8 to 1.0 percentage points to as low as 7 per cent. Although this is obviously good news for the investment property loan, the interest on your home loan has just fallen as well — by as much as $117 a month.

Linking an offset account

One of the potentially more valuable extras that isn't available with all loans is an offset account. An *offset account* works by allowing the borrower to have spare cash sitting in an account linked to the mortgage, with any savings in the offset account offsetting interest charged against the mortgage.

That means that if a borrower with a loan of $250,000 had $40,000 in a linked offset account, the lender would charge interest on only $210,000 ($250,000 – $40,000).

Banks usually only allow customers one offset account with a loan package. And, if you still have a home loan, that's the mortgage to which you should attach the offset account. Here's why: Even if rates are the same on both the home and the investment property, the interest on the home loan is not tax-deductible.

Paying ahead into a redraw account

Redraw accounts work similarly to offset accounts, with a few important differences. A *redraw* account contains money repaid early from a loan. If a borrower had repayments of $2,000 a month for her mortgage, but paid $3,000 a month for a year, she would have repaid an extra $12,000. Most lenders will now have that money sitting in a redraw account — an account that allows the borrower to redraw it when she wants to have the money. The act of redrawing may, or may not, have an associated bank fee.

As a property investor, you need to be wary about redraw accounts attached to your investment property loans. The Tax Office has declared that any principal repaid on an investment loan is deemed to have been permanently repaid. One investor couple known to Bruce put the $80,000 they'd cleared from the sale of their own home into the redraw account of one of their investment properties while they were waiting for their new home to be built. This meant that their $156,000 loan had been reduced to $76,000 for six months. But their accountant informed them that, although they could take the money back out of the loan account, they would now be able to claim interest only against $76,000, not $156,000.

If you have both a home loan and an investment property loan, you may want to consider having the redraw account attached to the home loan. Many borrowers use a redraw account as a way of hiding money away for a rainy day.

Other useful products

A lender may offer you a few other optional extras as part of a loan package if your total loan balance is attractive enough. Usually, the bank offers these credit products in the hope you'll misuse them, incurring interest. But use them well and you get the advantage of using the bank's money for free each month. Some useful products the banks may offer you include

🖊 **Credit cards:** In the wrong hands, credit cards can be a danger to financial health but, used correctly, they can save you money on your mortgage each month. Most credit cards come with an interest-free period, usually 44 or 55 days. If your card is paid off in full each month — therefore, incurring no interest — you've used the bank's money for free. For example, if you run up an average monthly bill of $3,000 on a credit card, and repay it during the interest-free period, $3,000 of your own cash is constantly earning or saving you money. If this money is held in an offset account that's linked to your home loan (for the options, refer to the section 'Linking an offset account' earlier in this chapter), you could be saving approximately $240 a year on your mortgage — 8 per cent of $3,000. But don't use a credit card this way unless you're positive that you're going to be able to pay off the full credit balance each month.

🖊 **Cheque accounts:** Cheque accounts and cheque books are increasingly less useful in Australia due to the widespread use of credit cards and electronic transactions. However, an account that allows you to write cheques for free can save the occasional fee.

🖊 **Fee-free transactional banking:** Banks often charge a multitude of fees for everyday banking. The main charges are monthly account-keeping fees (which can be up to $20 a month), foreign ATM fees (usually $1.50 to $2.50) and excess transaction fees (50 cents to $3).

Considering a Professional Package

Professional packages, often abbreviated to *pro-packs*, were originally designed as specially marketed packages for high-income earners, such as those in the medical, legal and accounting professions. Nowadays, however, pro-packs are available to anyone who does enough business with the bank — which usually simply means having a big enough loan or loans. Competition means that banks have continued to expand these offers and most borrowers find that for $300 or $500 a year they can have access to all the additional products offered (refer to the preceding section).

Two more features of most professional packages can be stand-out advantages to property investors. The first is that you get access to all these potentially useful products while also getting a discounted variable interest rate. A second advantage is that you often get free (or steeply discounted) loan-application fees in subsequent years. Loan-application fees can be $600 to $1,000 with many lenders. If you're intending to build a property portfolio, not having to pay a loan-application fee every time you purchase a property can compensate for the annual fee.

Qualifying for a pro-pack isn't difficult. Most banks start offering them at loans as low as $150,000. But bigger discounts usually kick in when your loans exceed $250,000.

Avoiding Some Big Hidden Nasties

Outside of the normal lending fees discussed earlier in this chapter, two major costs (potentially thousands of dollars each) you want to avoid, if possible, are lenders' mortgage insurance and exit fees. And you can avoid them under some circumstances within your control.

Lenders' mortgage insurance

An unusual and slightly nasty charge, *lenders' mortgage insurance (LMI)* is the bank getting you to pay the bank's insurance premium in case you default on the loan. The bank takes the risk, but you pay the premium for its insurance. The percentage rate charged for LMI rises exponentially in direct relation to the percentage of the property's cost you're seeking to borrow.

If you want to borrow less than 80 per cent of the purchase price of a property, you usually won't have to pay LMI. If you want to borrow slightly more than 80 per cent, you may find you have to pay only a few hundred dollars (or a fraction of a per cent of the entire loan's value). If you're borrowing 90 per cent or more of the value of the property, LMI will be thousands of dollars (or perhaps 1 to 2 per cent of the loan's value). If you're borrowing more than 95 per cent of the value of the property, you could pay tens of thousands of dollars (or 3 to 4 per cent of the loan's value).

However, banks take into account other equity you have in assets and loans you hold with them, if you're prepared to cross-collateralise your other loans or take out recourse loans (refer to

Chapter 4). If you're buying your first investment property, but already have substantial equity in your own home, you have a good chance of escaping LMI.

Here's an example of cross-collateralisation: A couple bought their house some years ago and have paid down some of their loan, while the value of their house has risen. Their house is now worth $600,000 and their loan has fallen to $200,000. They've found an investment property they want to buy for $450,000. They want to borrow the whole purchase price plus the settlement costs, up to another 5 to 6 per cent (refer to Chapter 3 for information on what you may need to borrow). The loan would be approximately $477,000, based on 6 per cent settlement costs.

Current loan position on home:

Home loan: $200,000

Home value: $600,000

Loan-to-value ratio (LVR) on the home: 33.3 per cent

Investment loan request:

Investment property loan: $477,000

Investment property value: $450,000

LVR on investment property alone: 106 per cent

Combined loans after investment property purchase:

Joint value of loans: $677,000

Joint value of properties: $1,050,000

LVR on joint property loans: 64.5 per cent

With the combined value of the loans as a percentage of the overall value of the properties less than 80 per cent, the bank is unlikely to charge LMI. Had the couple owed $480,000 on their home loan, the same example would bring an LVR of 91.1 per cent and LMI would have to be paid.

The good news on LMI is that, when it's charged by a bank, it's usually added to the loan amount. That is, a borrower may have tried to buy a $300,000 unit, plus all the extra settlement costs, for a $318,000 loan, but the LMI is added to the loan, so the loan becomes $323,000. Interest costs on servicing the LMI are, therefore, treated as a tax deduction (for investors).

Don't ever confuse LMI with *mortgage insurance*, which is a form of life insurance that a bank offers (usually as a monthly premium added to your mortgage) that will pay out your loan in the event of your death, leaving the property asset for your estate. Mortgage insurance is usually more expensive than normal life insurance, so the latter is usually preferable.

Exit fees

Exit fees were effectively banned by the federal government in mid-2011 to allow borrowers to be able to leave lenders charging interest rates that were unfair. Borrowers had long been concerned that they would get locked into a loan and not be able to leave a lender that was neither competitive nor providing good service. However, the new law has made big inroads on this and you can now much more easily leave a bank with which you're unhappy.

The ban on exit fees is not retrospective. If you have a loan that pre-dates 1 July 2011, you might still have to pay exit fees. Make sure you ask precisely what fees will be charged before you try to exit your loan.

The ban on exit fees doesn't mean you won't face any fees for leaving a bank, or that you won't still find moving banks difficult. The new bank, or the application process, may see you incur a new series of fees, including application fees and *mortgage discharge fees* (which are fees paid to the government for the registration of mortgage documents).

Even though exit fees are now banned on new loans, you should still ask your lender what fees you will incur if you need or wish to end the loan early. Ask the specific question: If I want to get out of this loan after one, three or five years, what extra costs will be incurred?

Attributing Rental Income

You'd think that rental income is rental income, right? If a tenant pays $1,300 a month to rent your investment property, you've received $1,300 in rent, correct?

No. Banks don't see it that way. Banks discount the rent that can be attributed to you as income, and the calculation differs from lender to lender. Depending on the lender's individual rules, she may allow you to attribute only between 60 and 80 per cent of that $1,300 to your income (for the purposes of deciding if you can afford the loan). That's somewhere between $780 and $1,040. Lenders' reasoning for making this calculation makes some sense. They realise that properties have ongoing expenses (see Chapter 7 for a rundown of ongoing property costs) and that the rent you receive won't all go towards your loan.

Note: The Tax Office doesn't see income and expenses the same way. They use actual income and actual expenses.

Ask your proposed lender how much of the rent you receive he'll allow to be attributed as net rental income. If the figure is substantially below 80 per cent, that lender may not be a great long-term partner for your property-investment future.

Solving Loan Predicaments

In Chapter 4, we discuss the different types of mortgages and how to select the one that best fits your situation. But remember that, just because you want a particular mortgage, doesn't mean you'll be approved for it.

The best defence against loan rejection is avoiding it in the first place. To head off potential rejection, disclose anything that may cause a problem *before* you apply for the loan. For example, if you already know your credit report indicates some late payments from when you were out of the country for an extended period or your family was in turmoil over a medical problem, write a letter to your lender that explains this situation. Or perhaps you're self-employed and your income from two years ago on your tax return was artificially much lower due to a special tax write-off. If that's the case, explain that in writing to the lender.

Even if you're the ideal mortgage borrower in the eyes of every lender, you may encounter financing problems with some properties. And, of course, not all real estate buyers have a perfect credit history, lots of spare cash and no debt. If you're one of those borrowers who must jump through more hoops than others to get a loan, don't give up hope. Few borrowers are perfect from a lender's perspective, and many problems aren't that difficult to fix.

Polishing your credit report

Late payments, missed payments or debts you've never bothered to pay can tarnish your credit report and squelch a lender's desire to offer you a mortgage. If you've been turned down for a loan because of your less-than-stellar credit history, you need to get a copy of your credit report to see if you can repair it.

We advise you to get a credit report before you even apply for a loan. In Australia, two organisations monitor applications for credit. Although banks pay to access the information, consumers can ask for free reports on their own credit history (they may charge for instant online requests). These organisations are Veda Advantage (go to www.mycreditfile.com.au — in the menu bar click on Personal, which brings up a link to order your report for free) and Dun & Bradstreet (www.checkyourcredit. com.au, where you want to request your personal credit report). The free reports take up to ten days to arrive via email or mail. If you see any errors on your report, contact the lender and get the mistake reviewed or explain why you have an issue with the report.

If problems are accurately documented on your credit report, try to explain them to your lender. Getting the bum's rush? Call other lenders and tell them your credit problems up-front and see whether you can find one willing to offer you a loan. Mortgage brokers will be valuable to help you shop for lenders in these cases.

Sometimes you may feel you're not in control when you apply for a loan. In reality, you can fix a number of credit problems yourself. And you can often explain those you can't fix. Some lenders are more lenient and flexible than others. Just because one mortgage lender rejects your loan application doesn't mean that all the others will.

As for erroneous information listed on your credit report, get on the phone to the credit bureaus. If specific creditors are the culprits, call them too. They're required to submit any new information or correct any errors at once. Keep notes from your conversations and make sure you put your case in writing and add your comments to your credit report. If the customer service representatives you talk with are no help, send a letter to the complaints department of each company. Getting mistakes cleaned up on your credit report can take the tenacity of a bulldog — be persistent.

Another common credit problem is having too much consumer debt at the time you apply for a mortgage. The more credit card, car loan and other consumer debt you rack up, the smaller the mortgage you're likely to qualify for. If you're turned down for the mortgage, consider it a wake-up call to get rid of this high-cost debt. Hang on to the dream of buying real estate and plug away at paying off your debts before you make another foray into real estate. (Refer to Chapter 3 for more information on entering the real estate market.)

Conquering insufficient income

If you're self-employed or have changed jobs, your income may not resemble your past income or, more importantly, your income may not be what a mortgage lender likes to see in respect to the amount you want to borrow. A simple (although not always feasible) way around this problem is to make a larger deposit. For example, if you put down 40 per cent when you purchase a rental property, you will have a much wider range of possible lenders for getting a loan. While low-documentation, or low-doc, loans were largely wiped out in 2011, if you can make that large a deposit, the income requirements to service the loan will fall considerably. Banks also know they'll simply be able to repossess and then sell your property if you default on the loan.

If you can't make a large deposit, another option is to get a guarantor for the loan — your relatives may be willing. As long as they aren't overextended themselves, they may be able to help you qualify for a larger loan than you can get on your own. As with partnerships, make sure you put your agreement in writing so that no misunderstandings occur. And understand that if you default, you're also putting the guarantor's finances at risk. Asking someone to be your guarantor isn't a request that should be asked lightly. And if the relative doesn't feel comfortable becoming a guarantor, that's your problem. You shouldn't make it his or hers.

Part III
Finding and Operating Properties

Glenn Lumsden

'It cost next to nothing and, if my calculations regarding global warming are correct, we'll have beachfront views by the time we retire.'

In this part ...

*H*ere's where the rubber hits the road. In this part, we discuss what, where and how to buy a rental property, what to take into account if you're looking at opportunities outside major metropolitan areas, and what tenants want. We cover some important information on how to value and evaluate real estate investment properties, including what to be wary of when taking on a previous investor's lease. In property investing, you aim to make money when you buy the property, so we arm you with how to source the information you need to reduce the chance you'll overpay. And, we cover the ongoing costs of property investment that you need to factor into your funding strategy.

Chapter 6

Location, Location, Value

• •

In This Chapter

▶ Choosing your investment area

▶ Looking at what makes a good investment area

▶ Analysing opportunities for tenant appeal

▶ Understanding city living

▶ Checking out regional and rural property

▶ Weighing up community attributes

• •

*A*s the most well-known saying in real estate goes, 'The three most important factors to success in real estate are location, location, location!' A strong correlation *does* exist between the location of your real estate investments and your financial success. And we firmly agree that the location of your real estate investment is critical in determining your success as a real estate investor. But we prefer Eric's phrase: 'Location, location, value'. This revised adage clearly emphasises location but also stresses the importance of finding good value for your investment dollar.

Merely owning real estate isn't the key to success in real estate investing; acquiring and owning the right real estate at the right price is how to build wealth. As you gain experience in real estate, you'll develop your own strategy, but to make any strategy succeed, you need to do your homework and diligently and fairly evaluate both the positive and negative aspects of your proposed real estate investment. That's where we come in.

In this chapter, we cover the important aspects of what makes metropolitan, regional and rural demographics different, how to analyse the economy and which factors are most important to property investing. We also discuss barriers to entry and the supply–demand equation. Then we show you where to find this information and how to interpret the numbers to determine your local areas with the most potential.

Deciding Where to Invest

If you're going to invest in real estate, you need to decide on a location. Most real estate investors initially look around their local communities. Bruce certainly doesn't recommend that you acquire investment property in the suburb you call home, or an adjoining suburb, because that would lack diversification — that is, if your home suburb is performing poorly, your investment property would be too. This applies particularly to those living in the smaller cities and towns outside of Australia's major state capitals.

If you live in a state capital city, that's probably where you may like to begin your search for potential investments. Knowing what's happening on the other side of the state capital city where you live is easier than knowing what's happening interstate, though we do discuss the many benefits of owning property interstate later in this chapter.

The vast majority of Australians live in the mainland state capitals of Melbourne, Sydney, Brisbane, Adelaide and Perth. The rest of Australia is pretty sparsely populated. And it's in those major cities — particularly Sydney, Melbourne and Brisbane — that more long-term stability and proven growth in property prices occurs. (See the section 'Australia's major property markets' later in this chapter for more on this.)

Although virtually everyone lives in an area with opportunities for real estate investing, not everyone lives in an area where the prospects are *good* for real estate in general. That's why it's important to broaden your geographic investment horizon.

Even if you decide to invest in real estate in your own area, you still need to do lots of research to decide where and what to buy — these are extremely important decisions with long-term consequences. In the sections that follow, we explain what to look for in a city or town before you make that investment decision. Keep in mind, though, that you can spend the rest of your life looking for the *perfect* real estate investment, never find it, never invest, and miss out on lots of opportunities, profit and even fun.

Evaluating a Region: The Big Picture

Though we advise you to consider your state capital, at least for your first property, any decision about where to invest should start with an evaluation of the overall economic viability and trends for that city. If the capital isn't economically sound, the likelihood for successful investments within that area is diminished. To buy right, you need to understand how to evaluate important economic data so that you can invest in the areas that are poised for growth.

We define those regions as the mainland *state* capitals of Australia — Sydney, Melbourne, Brisbane, Perth and Adelaide. Australia's smallest state capital, Hobart, and the two territory capitals, Canberra and Darwin, are generally very small markets, which can be overly affected by economic conditions or the decisions of governments.

Gathering and analysing the relevant economic data has never been easier, thanks to the internet. The most important data for population growth, job growth and economic trends is available online. From the federal government (the Australian Bureau of Statistics, at www.abs.gov.au, is a good source of this type of information), to state and local governments, to universities and business groups, information on economic trends is readily available.

Population growth

Population growth is one of the cornerstones upon which demand for real estate is based. An area with a steady growth in population is soon going to need more residential and commercial rental properties. More people mean more demand for housing, higher demand for retail shopping, and increased demand for offices and service providers. In other words, people use real estate, so the demand for real estate is enhanced as the population increases.

Increases or decreases in population are the result of three activities: births, deaths and people moving into or out of the area. Tremendous shifts in population have occurred from time to time, from the larger states of Victoria and New South Wales to higher growth states such as Queensland and Western

Australia. Immigration has also been a major factor in many parts of the country. In recent years, the shift to Western Australia and Queensland has been about the resources boom, which itself needs to be monitored. If the boom turns to bust, many of those workers who moved within Australia may shift back to their home towns.

How does population growth affect your real estate decisions? Simply put, economists theorise that a new household is needed for every increase in population of three people. Of course, these numbers can vary, based on average household size. However, if you're considering investments in rental homes or small apartment buildings in a certain area, the overall net population growth can be a factor in determining current and future demand for rental housing.

Job growth and income levels

Job growth is another fundamental element in determining demand for real estate. One measure economists often use is a belief that a new household is needed for every 1.5 jobs created. So if a new employer moves into the area and brings 150 new jobs, the local real estate housing market will need approximately 100 new dwelling units. Of course, these new jobs also positively affect the demand for commercial, industrial and retail properties.

The Australian Bureau of Statistics (ABS) compiles job growth and other economic data by state and region. This info is available at the ABS website (www.abs.gov.au).

You also need to know about the types of jobs people in an area are employed in before you can estimate their effect on the demand for each type of real estate. Although job growth is critical, so are the following factors:

- ✔ **Income levels:** Without stable, well-paying jobs, an area can stagnate. Even with positive growth in population and jobs, a low overall income level can stifle the demand for additional residential and commercial properties.

- ✔ **Level of employment diversification:** If the local economy is heavily reliant on jobs in a small number of industries, that dependence increases the risk of your real estate investments. Several large 'second cities', such as Geelong and Newcastle, are notable examples where the job market,

and hence real estate market, was once tied to the rising
and falling fortunes of some industries.

✔ **Industries represented:** If most of the jobs come from
shrinking employment sectors, such as farming, small
retail and manufacturing, real estate prices are unlikely to
rise quickly in the years ahead. On the other hand, areas
with high-growth industries, such as technology, often
stand a greater chance of faster price appreciation.

✔ **Types of jobs:** The specific types of jobs available can
be important, depending on the target market for your
property. If you're buying an office building in an urban
area, look for statistics on current and future employment
levels for professional employment. For example, owning
an office building across the street from a new courthouse
gives you a real advantage in attracting law firms and legal
support firms.

In addition to job growth, other good signs to look for include
the following:

✔ **Stable to increasing wages:** The demand for real estate
is clearly correlated to income levels, so local jobs with
strong underlying demand are key. With many jobs being
outsourced to other parts of the country and around the
world, it's important that the local jobs are not only secure,
but also unlikely to see an erosion in purchasing power.

✔ **A recession-resistant employment base:** Traditionally,
jobs that enjoy stability are in the fields of education,
government and medical services. Even areas renowned for
strong demand and limited supply of real estate can slow
down if the economy is hit hard.

✔ **Declining unemployment:** Examine how the jobless rate
has changed in recent years. You wouldn't want to invest
your savings in a rental property located next to a large
typewriter factory!

Investigating Your Intended Real Estate Market

With real estate investing, deciding where to invest is frequently
more important than choosing the specific rental property. You
can have a rental property that meets the needs of the market,
but if it's located in a declining area where the demand is weak

or in an area that has been overbuilt with an excess of available properties, your investment won't perform financially. (These are the properties that perform the worst over time but are typically the types of properties highly touted by property seminar spruikers, who love to brag about how much real estate they control but rarely tell you about their long-term investment returns.)

Likewise, you need to determine the areas that may be too richly priced, because your cash flow and future appreciation will be hurt if you overpay for a property. Often, properties in the best neighbourhoods in town are so overpriced that they may fall considerably in the short term.

Australia's major property markets

According to the ABS measures of *statistical divisions*, more than 60 per cent of the population lives in Australia's mainland state capitals — Sydney, Melbourne, Brisbane, Perth and Adelaide. So, it should go without saying that more than half of the real estate opportunities in this country are in those cities.

Unlike the United States, from where Eric and Robert hail, Australia has only five cities with populations of more than one million. Even if you reduce the minimum threshold to a population of 500,000, you only add another two cities to the list (Gold Coast–Tweed Heads and Newcastle).

The importance of Australia's mainland capital cities in real estate markets outweighs just their 60 per cent weighting of the population. They also tend to be better real estate markets in which to invest because of their relative stability. As you read through the following sections of this chapter, take note of exactly how the economic factors we cover apply to real estate in, particularly, these five capital cities.

The main reason that the mainland state capitals offer the most opportunities revolves around the diversification offered via the volume of industries and employers. (We have nothing against Hobart! It's a beautiful capital, though small by Australian standards.) Although Perth is highly susceptible to the health of the resources and mining sectors, the West's capital has many other major industries that employ significant numbers of people. So diversification of industries means more employment options.

Melbourne — and the other major state capitals — is large because significant headquarters for Australia's largest government, manufacturing, banking, telecommunications, health care, information technology, mining and resources, and utilities sectors are based there. Where the headquarters for these industries lie outside of metropolitan areas, they are often the major employer and bring major employer risk with them.

As opposed to the major state capitals, most of the smaller towns in rural and regional Australia have one or two large businesses that dominate employment in the town. If that employer went broke, or decided to relocate to another area, the impact on the town's economy could be devastating.

Although Bruce believes that it is possible to make good returns from property anywhere in Australia, significantly enhanced risks are involved with investing outside of the major state capitals. Bruce would never say 'Don't do it', but he does warn that you need to be acutely aware of the health of not just a small local economy, but the major employers within that economy — something that's less relevant in major metropolises.

Later in this chapter, we delve further into the benefits and risks of metropolitan and non-metropolitan properties.

Supply and demand

The supply and demand for real estate in a given market has a direct impact on the financial performance of your investment property. And, although we firmly believe that the overall economic prospects of a city are vital, you must also find supply and demand information about the specific type of real estate that you plan to purchase.

Obviously, the best environment for investing in real estate is one with strong demand and limited supply. When demand exceeds supply, shortages of available real estate occur.

Both sides of the equation — supply and demand — have indicators you want to evaluate in forming your consensus about the strength of the local market. *Supply-side indicators* include building permits, the rate at which new properties have been rented or absorbed into the market and the availability of alternatives for similar real estate. *Demand indicators* include occupancy and rent levels.

Before we look at different types of indicators in detail, you need to know how they work together:

- ✔ The overall relationship between supply and demand determines the market conditions for real estate. For example, a large number of pending or recently issued building permits, weak *absorption*, or rental, of new properties and an excess of rental-property listings that have been on the market for an extended time are all indicators that the supply of a specific product type is greater than the demand. Such market conditions will soon result in lower occupancy, lower rents and, occasionally, concessions like free rent or lower rental rates early in the lease, which mean lower cash flow and smaller capital appreciation potential. These aren't the markets you should be seeking.

- ✔ When the demand for real estate is high, vacancies are few and property owners move to raise rents and remove any incentives, such as discounted rent, that were earlier offered to attract tenants. In commercial properties, landlords cut back on the building-improvement expenses and require the tenants to take the space as-is and make any upgrades or changes to the space at their own expense.

Building permits

Building permits are often the first tangible step outlining the intent of developers to build new real estate projects. Therefore, the number of building permits issued is an essential leading indicator to future supply of real estate.

The trend in the number of building permits tells you how the supply of real estate properties may soon change. A long and sustained rise in permits over several years can indicate that the supply of new property may dampen future price appreciation. In 2008, during the credit crisis, major banks drastically cut their lending to high-rise, inner-city apartments due to oversupply. When banks cut the percentage they're prepared to lend on a property, which they do infrequently, you can take this as a sign that they believe property prices for those types of properties in those areas are overpriced.

Availability of alternatives — renting versus buying

When the cost of buying is relatively low compared with the cost of renting, more renters can afford to purchase, thus increasing the number of home sales and lowering demand for rentals.

A key indicator you can use to gauge the market is the number of property listings, as follows:

✔ **Increase in property listings:** Increasing numbers of property listings is an indication of future trouble for real estate price appreciation. When the market is flooded with listings, prospective buyers can be choosier, exerting downward pressure on prices.

✔ **Decrease in property listings:** A sign of a healthy real estate market is a decreasing and low level of property listings, which indicates that the area's existing residents are content where they are and aren't inclined to move or sell. At high prices (relative to the cost of renting), more prospective buyers elect to rent and the number of sales relative to listings drops.

Vacancy rates

The vacancy rate is another way to gauge the supply and demand for a given property type in the local market. The *vacancy rate* for a particular type of property is the percentage of that type of property available for rent. For example, you may find data telling you that a local market has 2,312 rental properties in total, with 70 available for rent. That means a vacancy rate of 3 per cent.

Before you invest, determine the current occupancy levels for your proposed type of property. Simply ask a few local real estate agents these questions and aggregate the results. First, how many properties do they manage? Second, how many are currently vacant?

Rental levels

The trend in *rental rates* that renters are willing and able to pay over the years also gives a good indication as to the supply–demand relationship for property. When the demand for real estate just keeps up with the supply of housing and the local economy continues to grow, rents normally increase. This increase is a positive sign for continued capital appreciation.

On the Block: Metropolitan Properties

Australia is a very large country with a relatively small population, concentrated largely in metropolitan areas, the majority of which hug the edges of the continent. Most property-investment opportunities, therefore, are in the mainland state capital cities. That's not where *all* investment opportunities are, but it's where more than 60 per cent or so of Australians live, as discussed earlier in this chapter.

In the next few sections, we discuss the relative merits and risks associated with different kinds of locations. We look at the types of properties that you can find in each area, and give you an overview of the sorts of people who tend to live there.

Inner city

When we say inner city, we really mean within a small distance — up to 10 kilometres, depending on the size of the city — of the central business district (CBD) of the major Australian state capitals: Adelaide, Brisbane, Melbourne, Perth and Sydney.

Supply and demand dictates that inner-city properties will always be the most expensive. On the supply side, for a start, fewer properties are available in the inner city. If you draw a circle on a map with a 5-kilometre radius from the CBD, the area is, obviously, more limited than the area in a circle drawn, say, 15 or 20 kilometres from the CBD. On the demand side, inner-city properties have what people are prepared to pay more for — they're closer to corporate head offices, entertainment venues, regular public transport, older private schools and universities. That is to say, those living in the inner city often choose to do so because it cuts their travel time to and from employment or schools to a minimum. The low-supply, high-demand equation causes inner-city properties to have higher prices.

For exactly the same reasons, some other trends that separate what's available in the city, compared with further out in the suburbs, are

> ✓ **Rents tend to be higher.** People who don't want to buy, or can't afford to, are often prepared to pay to rent a place in the inner suburbs for the same reason others buy — the proximity to major city employment opportunities and attractions.

> ✔ **Properties tend to be smaller.** The higher rents are often for much smaller places. A small three-bedroom terrace house within a 20-minute walk to the CBD could cost twice as much per week as a three-bedroom, freestanding home on a big block of land 20 kilometres out. Demand for space means that apartments are more common in the city and houses are more common in the suburbs.

Suburban

Not everyone can afford to live in the inner city. More importantly, not everyone *wants* to live in the inner city. Some don't like the unclean air. Some hate the noise. Or, perhaps it's the traffic, the congestion on the footpaths and the fact that finding grass to put beneath your feet may require you to first take a 20-minute walk. Safety aspects, for children, pets or yourself, also come into it.

The fact is the suburbs are where most people happily choose to live. And that's something to remember when you buy an investment property (despite what some property experts say). In any state capital, more than 80 or 90 per cent of residents live outside a 5-kilometre radius of the CBD.

Seek and You Shall Find: The Sea, Ski or Tree Change

The turn-of-the-millennium ABC television show *SeaChange* can probably claim some of the credit for causing the recent shift by baby boomers to a lifestyle away from the cities. But, even if it can't, the show's name was certainly responsible for the coining of the phrase that's now a permanent part of Australian vocabulary.

Obviously, people were living in regional and rural areas long before baby boomers began their wind-down into retirement. But the impact of the baby boomers' shift can't be underestimated. Along with a generally wealthier population that values having a holiday home, it's caused house-price inflation in areas outside of state capitals, along Australia's immense coastline and in other 'greener pastures'.

Heading for the coast

Whether it's a shack or a mansion, owning a beachside house is a widely held dream in Australia. If your beach house is an investment, it can be a canny way of making money from understanding others' inclination to pay people rent for short stays at the coast.

The outcome of owning property beside the sea depends on what you're trying to achieve. If you're all about buying a holiday home for the family to enjoy on weekends and holidays, forget about it being an investment and enjoy. You can probably use the same sorts of criteria that you used to purchase your own home. That is, a place that fulfils your family's needs.

If the purchase is about investment and making money, you need to consider more risks than with the purchase of a property in a major city.

When coastal property is in fashion, more often than not the general economy is strong and people have spare money to indulge in a long-held dream to own a beachside place. But when the economy is weak — when corporations are culling jobs and the share market has taken an extended downturn — one of the first things to go when people hit tough times is the beach house. They can't afford two mortgages anymore and opt to keep their full-time home.

Regional and rural hideaways

Regional and rural properties are no shrinking violets in terms of investor interest and capital-price performance. Australians continue to spend money on holidays, and some of those dollars are spent on traditional driving holidays that can lead anywhere.

This pattern creates business opportunities in some smaller cities and country towns. Townspeople and those looking for a lifestyle or work change have opened up guesthouses offering bed and breakfast (B&Bs), where the host cooks a traditional fry-up for you in the morning, or simply services the house before and after a stay. Normal houses, flats and units can also be rented out for a night, a few days or a week or two in some locations where strong weekend demand, in particular, exists.

Comparing Communities Come Investment Time

The reputation of particular communities can be based on many factors, but certain key or essential elements differentiate the neighbourhoods with good reputations and positive trends from the areas that are stagnant or trending in the wrong direction.

Schools

If you don't have school-age children, you may not initially be concerned about the reputation of local schools in a region. Think again. Whether you're investing in residential or commercial properties, schools matter. The demand for residential and commercial property (and the subsequent value of the property) is correlated to the quality of local schools.

Ask any real estate agent about the impact of schools on the demand and sales price for a home in a great school district. Likewise, employers use the quality of local schools to recruit personnel.

Public transport

Not everyone owns a car and many people who do don't want to drive to work. Some of the key reasons commuters choose public transport over taking their cars, particularly in metropolitan areas, include the costs associated with running a car, the costs of parking in the city, and the relative stress-free travel of public transport.

The closer a suburb is to the heart of the city, the better the public transport network tends to be. Population density plays a huge role here, but the point we want to make is this: Inner-city residents who take public transport get access to more regular services, which allows them to get around with ease. This factor enhances a community.

Amenities

Amenities are important to many tenants. These include the availability of reasonable shopping precincts, hospitals and government services. Some suburbs have been overlooked by governments over the years, for one reason or another, and provide minimal services and, therefore, fewer incentives for people to live in the area.

Federal, state and local government amenities include services for families and the elderly, such as public libraries, childcare, schools, hospitals, government-sponsored employment services and sporting facilities — parks, football ovals and swimming pools. All these facilities not only provide much-needed services for local communities, but also create a source of employment for locals.

The availability of a shopping district is just as important. Everyone needs to shop regularly for food and clothes. And don't underestimate the pulling power of restaurants. The modern Australian lifestyle includes eating out more often — both for the food and socialising.

Crime rates

Crime can have a significant and sobering effect on the demand and desirability of all types of properties. No-one wants to live in a high-crime area, and commercial tenants and their customers will neither work at nor patronise unsafe businesses. No areas are going to be crime-free, but you don't want to find out after settlement that you've purchased a rental property at the epicentre of the local drug trade.

Pride of ownership

Pride of ownership is an intangible attitude that has tangible results. Pride of ownership also has no economic boundaries — even modest-income areas can really look sharp.

 Look for investment properties in communities that reflect pride of ownership — well-kept, litter-free grounds, trimmed plants, beautiful flowers, fresh paint and so on. This is the kerb appeal that helps you attract and retain your tenants.

You can control the appearance, condition and maintenance of your own property, but your options are limited if the properties surrounding yours fall into disrepair.

Chapter 7

The Ongoing Costs of Real Estate

In This Chapter

▶ Preparing for expected and unexpected expenses

▶ Being aware of government taxes

▶ Dealing with other costs — utilities, agents, improvements and insurance

● ●

*U*nlike almost any other asset class, direct property ownership is an investment that the words 'set and forget' do not apply to. If you buy blue-chip shares, so the saying goes, you can 'put the share certificate in the bottom draw and pull it out in 20 years to retire'. The holding time for property may be similar — most real estate investment should be for the long haul — but a hands-off approach isn't possible in direct property investment. And one of the many reasons for that is that property, unlike other asset classes, has a large number of expenses and management issues that require ongoing consideration.

Ongoing costs are part and parcel of property investment. Although the income stream from property (rent) is usually fairly even, the expenses side of the equation is less so. Some bills come monthly or quarterly. Some can be annual. But plenty of bills can come crashing down out of nowhere. And they simply must be paid. Taking the 'lumpy' nature of property costs into account when putting together your finances can save plenty of heartache down the track. From the mortgage to maintenance and body corporate fees, to ongoing property taxes, utility charges, agents' fees, property improvements and even insurance, this chapter tells you about the range of property costs that you need to budget for.

Budgeting for the Inevitable

Managing real estate investments is a slimmed-down version of managing your own business. If you've bought the property on your own or with your spouse (which is how most investment property is bought), your property is your business and you need to be involved in making the decisions. Some of the decisions are small and can be left to people you employ, if you so wish, but some decisions are major and you wouldn't want hired help to make them for you.

Even if you've employed a real estate agent to do some of the work for you and an accountant to do some other parts of the work for you, they will always come back to you when the big decisions need to be made. The big decisions are inevitably about big costs — particularly where an item has given up the ghost and must be replaced.

In the following sections, we cover some of the expenses you need to budget for.

Mortgage interest — month in, month out

For most property investments, the single biggest ongoing expense is the interest on the mortgage, certainly in the first few years if most of the purchase price was financed with a loan. In many cases, this expense alone can soak up all the rent received and some of your personal income. The good news is that interest paid on money borrowed is, in most cases, tax-deductible, meaning that it can be claimed against your income.

Interest costs are also one of the few costs that are likely to fluctuate significantly from year to year. Interest costs are linked to the interest rates set by the Reserve Bank of Australia (RBA). If the RBA is lifting rates because it's trying to control inflation or because the economy is picking up strength, interest costs can increase significantly. Conversely, if inflation is considered to be low or benign and the RBA is concerned about the economy slowing too much, rates can fall fairly quickly.

 For all the media interest and focus on the issue, the RBA doesn't change interest rates all that often. In the financial year to 30 June 2012, four interest rate cuts occurred. Only one movement (which moved interest rates up) occurred in the 2011 financial year. Of course, the RBA was reasonably active following the GFC, as it actively tried to manage Australia's economy. Six moves occurred each year in the 2010 and 2009 financial years and four in 2008.

Australian borrowers have been far more at the mercy of Australian banks since the GFC. The GFC was, in reality, a credit crisis. And the 'cost of lending' for Australian banks, which source some of the money to lend to Australians from offshore, increased dramatically. Since early 2008, Australian banks have moved their interest rates often independently of the RBA's official cash rate, even though that is the direct cost for a portion of their funding.

Over the course of any investment property loan held for longer than a year, interest rates will both rise and fall. Keep track of your bank statements, because making sure you claim your legal entitlements to costs such as interest expenses is a considerable factor in determining the financial success of your investment property.

Financing unpredictable maintenance issues

Question: How can you plan for a heating or cooling system conking out? A toilet that now refuses to flush? Or a keyhole rusting over? How about burst water pipes? **Answer:** You can't really. Whether you've previously lived in your parents' home, a rental property or a home you bought and have lived in for some time, you probably have firsthand experience that property-maintenance issues are unpredictable at best and, at worst, perfectly timed to cause maximum financial distress.

If you have a large investment property with multiple residential tenants or a commercial property with a full-time manager, many potential issues can or will be caught as they arise or before they become a serious issue. But, usually, when looking after your first investment property, most maintenance issues aren't going to become obvious until they've actually gone beyond the 'maintenance' stage and on to the 'repair or replace' stage. Some maintenance issues can be looked at semi-regularly — such as before each new tenant moves in or every few years with an ongoing tenant.

One way of finding out where some maintenance issues or structural problems may be hiding, especially before you buy a property, is to hire a professional builder to conduct a *pre-purchase inspection* report (for more information about property inspections, see Chapter 8). A building expert is able to point out major faults and potential structural-maintenance issues that could, or should, be looked at over the short term — one, two or three years. In some instances, the report may sway you against buying that property at all, or could give you leverage to negotiate the final purchase price. But even the experts can't predict the remaining life span of some of the bigger and important items.

When discussing financing regular property costs and 'lumpy' property costs, the biggest concern for a first-time property investor is, 'How much do I need to have available for these sorts of emergencies?' Unfortunately, no simple answer is possible. However, you can use the following list to help figure out what you may need:

✔ **Is the house old or new?** Older period-style houses are understandably likely to be more expensive to maintain, because more of the items in them are older and closer to the end of their use-by date.

✔ **Has the property been renovated recently?** Especially for older properties, does it look like the current owner has been doing work to update the property? If the house has things like freshly polished floorboards, a new garden, an updated bathroom, kitchen or laundry, it's possible they got a contractor to fix up a few other problems at the same time.

✔ **Are the fixtures and fittings in the house old?** Have a look at items such as ovens, toilets, air conditioners, gas heaters, exhaust fans, hot-water systems and household taps to see how well they've been maintained or how recently they've been replaced.

One of the most important things you can do is ask questions. If you're buying the property to lease out to tenants immediately — that is, you're not buying the property to knock it down and rebuild — ask the agent selling the property to find out when major structural work was last done or when things were last attended to. Not relevant for every property but, if necessary, ask about restumping, rewiring, reroofing and replumbing. When were these jobs done and by whom? If the agent can show you receipts, all the better.

Here's a good standard for first-time property investors: Set aside (or, at the very least, ensure you can easily access) $2,000 or $3,000 to fund small emergency maintenance or structural work.

Be aware of tax implications that may also apply to maintaining your property. The Australian Taxation Office (ATO) has specific rules about what an investor can claim deductions for in the first year of ownership. The rules are designed to restrict obvious maintenance costs from effectively being passed on to the taxpayer. In some cases, early repairs and maintenance may need to be treated as a capital expense and depreciated over a number of years, rather than claimed as an up-front deduction.

Real estate agent management of maintenance costs

If a real estate agent is to manage your property, be aware that most basic rental agreements give the agent the authority to approve urgent repairs up to a limit of $1,000. This arrangement is to cover most true emergencies that affect the ongoing enjoyment of the property by the tenant — hot-water systems breaking down, problems with heating or cooling systems, and leaking pipes or toilets. In most cases, the real estate agent uses a contractor, who bills the agent, and then the real estate agent bills you.

If the work is less than the rent the agent collects for you each month, in most cases the agent will take the charge out of your next month's rent and pass on any remaining rent as normal.

Funding major maintenance issues

Bigger and more expensive maintenance work is not uncommon. If a particularly expensive problem emerges — such as the realisation that the roof really must be replaced immediately or the bathroom, kitchen or laundry needs to be renovated before leasing out to tenants — then it could be time to go to the bank to get funding.

In a few situations, borrowing money for maintenance work may be your best option. If you have a very large item that requires repair, you may want to ask the bank to extend your current property loan to cover the expense, particularly if you don't have the ready cash. You may also be able to claim a tax deduction on the interest on the loan. Before you call on the bank, however, keep in mind that you need to be in a position to borrow cash, particularly if you don't have much equity in the property (or equity in other assets over which your bank has a mortgage).

Body corporate fees

Most apartments or units are governed by a *body corporate* (to an extent determined by the laws of the state in which the property is located), comprising all owners of individual units within the block.

Several laws govern the existence of bodies corporate, designed to cover everything from blocks of several hundred apartments to a subdivided property with joint use of land. The main purpose of a body corporate is to take control of the maintenance of common property, usually the external areas of the buildings and shared grounds and facilities, and issues that affect many or all of the owners of properties that are adjoined or share a building lot. Some bodies corporate simply get together once a year to determine if any issues exist that require a vote. Legal requirements vary from state to state for the responsibilities of a body corporate but, normally, a body corporate must have a committee, hold committee meetings and an annual general meeting, and ensure that the public liability insurance for common areas is up to date.

One of the main duties of a body corporate is to look after joint maintenance issues — gardening, external painting and cleaning, and so on. These items are paid for through funds raised from the owners of the properties. The day-to-day maintenance issues are usually covered by a body corporate administration fund. Bigger complexes may also have a building or sinking fund for major capital works.

In most cases, both of these funds require regular contributions from owners so that enough money is available to deal with maintenance issues over time. Regular contributions of several hundred dollars (or more) a year or a quarter are put aside so that major maintenance projects can be attended to when required or scheduled.

Before you buy a property that may have a body corporate attached to it, make sure you find out the exact status of its finances. Also, make sure you read the body's governing document. Bodies corporate that have administration funds or building/sinking funds that are broke, that have trouble collecting dues from their owners, or have a long list of items that look like they should have been attended to some time ago, could be a warning to keep clear of the property. Before buying in, find out exactly what you'll be required to pay each quarter or each year and what work has been planned and costed that will require you to put your hand in your pocket. Some body corporate items still come out of the blue but, by doing your research, you may be able to reduce the impact of unexpected financial shocks.

Ongoing Property Taxes

Governments at all levels have their fingers all over real estate. A few big taxes are levied up-front, such as stamp duty to state governments (refer to Chapter 3) and the 10 per cent GST on property construction to the federal government. And, of course, you have annual income tax return commitments. But you'll also find a few other less well known taxes that you may need to pay regularly and should be aware of.

Council rates

Rates are levied by individual councils and shires across Australia to pay for services provided to residents, such as rubbish collection, the building of footpaths and bicycle tracks, street cleaning, parking management, tree trimming, the maintenance of public gardens and traffic maintenance (which are important to the upkeep of your house and your street). Rates can also contribute to local community organisations, such as parents' groups, senior citizens' groups and family care centres (all of which may be of interest to your tenants). Unlike stamp duty and land tax, discussed in the next section, at least you get something directly in return for ongoing council rates. In some states, councils or council-run bodies are also the providers of some utility services, including water, drainage and sewerage (for more information on these services, see 'Utility charges' later in this chapter).

Every council has its own method of determining the actual rate to be levied on individual properties. In most cases, the amount is worked out according to the value of the property — that is, higher value properties pay proportionately more in council rates than lower value properties.

Do they know where you are?

After you've settled on a property, double-check that the local council is aware of your current contact details — otherwise, you could be saddled with a big fat bill later on, as Bruce once was. The local council of a property that Bruce had bought was given out-of-date contact details for him at settlement by his conveyancing team. The council sent rates notices to the out-of-date address twice, but the notices were returned to sender. The rates continued to accumulate with penalty interest.

The council made no further attempt to contact Bruce — not even by sending a letter to the address of the investment property, where a tenant or agent might have noticed it — and he didn't notice that he wasn't paying a bill he had never received. Eventually, Bruce realised he hadn't been paying rates and contacted the council himself. After about two years of ownership, the bill came to more than $3,000.

Rates are usually levied annually in advance. How those rates can be paid is determined by individual councils. Two main options are usually available:

 ✔ **Pay quarterly in advance:** The council sends you a rates notice once a quarter letting you know when the bill is due to be paid.

 ✔ **Pay annually:** The council may offer a second option, allowing you to pay the notice around halfway through the billing year, so that some is paid in arrears and some is paid in advance.

The previous owner has likely paid council rates in advance, covering a proportion of the post-settlement period, requiring the new property owner to reimburse the previous owner for that expense. The amount owing is usually calculated during the conveyancing process and the payment made during settlement.

Land tax

Land tax is another charge levied by state governments and the Australian Capital Territory. At the time of writing, the Northern Territory doesn't have a land tax. Like stamp duty (refer to Chapter 3), no obvious or direct benefit flows on to the person being charged the tax. Land tax is a regressive wealth tax designed to target property investors specifically. To that end, land tax is usually not levied on a person's principal place of residence (the family home), but is levied on all other landholdings within a state.

Land tax is an annual tax that's charged differently in every state. In some states, it's not levied until a property owner has land valued above a specified amount. When that ceiling has been breached, land tax then becomes payable on the value of all remaining land held by the investor in that state. The land value under that limit is never taxed. And that's an important point. Land tax is levied on the value of the land held by the investor, not the value of the property (which includes buildings and capital improvements) itself.

 For details of exactly how land tax is charged in your state or territory, contact your local state revenue office or department of treasury. The following list of website addresses can help you get started:

- ✔ **Australian Capital Territory:** www.revenue.act.gov.au/land_tax

- ✔ **New South Wales:** www.osr.nsw.gov.au

- ✔ **Queensland:** www.osr.qld.gov.au/land-tax

- ✔ **South Australia:** www.revenuesa.sa.gov.au

- ✔ **Tasmania:** www.sro.tas.gov.au

- ✔ **Victoria:** www.sro.vic.gov.au

- ✔ **Western Australia:** www.finance.wa.gov.au

As an investor, you can't do a lot to escape land tax if you're investing in one state or territory. At lower levels, land taxes, when they kick in, can be as little as a few hundred dollars. Owners of big commercial properties, however, may need to pay tens of thousands of dollars a year. Big city office buildings might be slugged hundreds of thousands of dollars a year.

 You can escape paying land tax by buying property in different states. For example, if you own four small properties in Victoria, you may well end up breaching the state's $250,000 threshold and have to pay land tax. However, if you own two properties in Victoria, two in New South Wales (where the limit is $396,000)

and three in Queensland (where the limit is $600,000), plus potentially others in other states, you might not be caught under any land tax net.

Other Costs to Be Aware Of

Investment properties incur a number of costs additional to the inevitable charges of mortgage interest, rates and taxes. You need to also budget for some utilities, the cost of managing the property, improvements to keep the market value growing, insurance and, in some instances, even garden maintenance.

Utility charges

The past two decades have seen much headway in transferring the costs associated with utility usage to the people responsible for the actual usage — tenants. In the 1990s, state governments began introducing legislation to encourage (or in some cases to make it compulsory) for landlords to install individual meters on most new properties (and some older developments) so that usage of water, electricity and gas could be measured by the individual unit forming part of a block. When that occurred and tenants had to start paying for their own usage instead of landlords paying, usage dropped dramatically.

Usage charges are, therefore, now largely paid by tenants. In circumstances where individual meters aren't installed, the landlord is still required to pay for those charges where they can't be separated. Where individual meters are connected, electricity, gas and water usage are charged directly by the utility company to the tenant.

The utility cost that's still usually levied to the property owner is non-usage charges for water. The provision of the water service, sewerage service and drainage is still generally levied to the landlord.

Agents' fees

One of the biggest ongoing fees associated with property investment is the cost of employing an agent. Agents in Australia tend to charge a percentage of the rent to manage your property. What you get for your monthly fee varies enormously, as does the quality of letting or leasing agents.

Agents' economies of scale

Although nothing is wrong with opting to manage your own property, Bruce doesn't recommend you do so if you're a first-time property investor, or an investor who owns only one or two properties. Here's why.

The average cost of employing an agent for an Australian property is about $1,200 to $1,300 a year (based on rent of $340 a week, times 52 weeks, times 7 per cent). For that price, you get a professional, or a team, who knows the many laws that govern running properties in your state. Usually, the agent knows what to do, has experience in doing it and has the systems in place to do it quickly. If a problem with a tenant arises, an agent can quickly organise the paperwork to get to the right tribunal to sort the matter, because it's something agents occasionally have to do. If an emergency occurs in the middle of the night or on a long weekend, agents know immediately which tradespeople will take the call. They also know a few

tricks when it comes to getting tenants to pay outstanding rent (although they're certainly not perfect in that regard). Think of the time you might spend collecting rent, even if you own only two properties in different parts of your city. Agents also have a good idea of what the local properties are renting for and how much your property is worth. For $1,200 a year, you usually get pretty good value (even for average-quality agents).

On the other hand, managing your own properties may make sense if you run a significant portfolio, own a block of apartments or have plenty of available time and the interest to become acquainted with the laws and processes you need to follow. If you own four properties, at a minimum, then you might save yourself $5,000 to $6,000 a year. The knowledge you need is no different for one property than it is for four. And you may be able to benefit from the economies of scale that professional agents have.

The base fee charged by agents is usually between 5.5 and 8.8 per cent of the rent (including the 10 per cent GST). Fees are usually higher for short-term rental properties, such as holiday homes and weekend rentals. For full-time tenanted properties, if your monthly rent is around $1,470 (the equivalent of $340 a week), your agent generally charges you between $81.00 and $129.65 a month to look after your property. Most months, for most properties, all the agent has to do for that fee is ensure somebody at the front counter provides the tenant with a written receipt for payment of rent (although rents and receipts are increasingly being looked after electronically). The agent is also responsible for chasing up the rent if the tenant forgets to pay or has trouble paying (although the property owner also needs to keep an eye on the agent when things get patchy). When everything is going smoothly, the tenant is paying on time and the property is holding itself together, agents seem to be overpaid. But when something goes wrong, having an agent to organise repairs, deal with tenants and attend court can be the cheapest employment contract you've ever signed. For more information on the services agents provide and what they charge for those services, see Chapter 8.

Some very good agents out there charge at the lower end of the scale and some very bad ones charge top dollar. Price isn't necessarily any indication of quality. The fees associated with agents are usually tax-deductible.

Property improvements

Properties require regular updating. Not every year and not for every tenant, but every now and then a property needs to be spruced up. If you want to get the best market rents, sometimes you need to splash on a coat of paint, modernise some of the fixtures and fittings, replace carpet and curtains, or even give an entire room or two a new feel.

Although you can easily research what each of these items cost, what's important to know is how they're treated in relation to tax. Most of the other ongoing expenses covered in this chapter (including agents' fees, land tax, council rates, body corporate fees, utility charges, gardening and insurance) can be claimed in the same year that the expense occurred. That's not necessarily the case with physical improvements to the home.

Some improvements are seen as repairs and maintenance and some are categorised as *capital improvements*. The difference is important, because it determines the speed with which you can claim the item's cost in your tax return. As a broad rule, big items need to be depreciated over many years, whereas small items can be claimed against the investor's income in the year the expense occurred. If you need to replace one venetian blind that costs $200, you may be able to claim that in tax in the year it's purchased (thereby getting a return according to your marginal tax rate). But a new dishwasher will probably have to be depreciated over a number of years.

Insurance

Don't consider starting out in real estate investment if you aren't prepared to be properly covered with insurance. Property assets are usually very big and expensive assets, and having one burn down or devastated by a storm can set you back years (maybe decades) if the house isn't properly insured.

Being a property investor, you'd be foolish to go without various types of insurance. The first and most obvious is *house and contents* insurance — to ensure the building can be rebuilt if it's wiped out by the aforementioned disasters. Make sure the insurance covers the fixtures and fittings (so you don't end up short of money to carpet the place and put window furnishings in).

Several providers in Australia also offer *landlord's* insurance. This allows an investor to cover lost rent if the house becomes uninhabitable for various reasons or if you get the tenant from hell. Both house and contents insurance and landlord's insurance are options designed to protect the property itself, and are fully tax-deductible.

Next up is the group of life insurance products that are more about insuring yourself and your family to make sure that the investment property strategy you're developing doesn't have to be cancelled should one of life's disasters happen to you. You want to consider four products: life insurance, total and permanent disablement insurance, trauma insurance and income-protection insurance. The first three pay a lump sum in the event of, respectively, your death, an injury that makes you no longer capable of working, and a traumatic illness (such as heart attack, stroke or cancer). Income-protection insurance insures a portion of your income in case illness or an accident stops you from working for an extended period.

Gardens

If your investment property is a house and you find a tenant who looks after the garden, you've found a rare tenant indeed. Tenants are notoriously unreliable when it comes to looking after the outside of the house they're living in. Many, in fact, believe it's not their responsibility, even though their rental agreements usually state that they should be maintaining the garden, including weeding and watering (with a mind, of course, to local water restrictions). Unless you've got a long-term and gardening-inclined family living in your property, your tenants are unlikely to even own a lawnmower, whipper snipper or a pair of secateurs, and are even less likely to go out and buy some.

You have the option to do the gardening yourself, but you would need to come to some arrangement with the tenant. Strictly speaking, a property manager or owner must allow the peaceful enjoyment of a tenanted property, which means that tenants must be given proper warning of any visits (for more information about legal responsibilities of owners and managers, see Chapter 8). This requires you writing to them to give them advance notice every time you want to go around and pull out a few weeds.

The good news is that, if you can't convince your tenants to do their duty, hiring a gardener is also a tax deduction.

The responsibility for gardens at multi-unit developments is usually addressed by the property's body corporate. In some cases, tenants may wish to look after small patches themselves, but the general rule is that gardening expenses come out of funds levied by the body corporate (for more information, refer to 'Body corporate fees' earlier in this chapter).

Chapter 8

Landlording 101

· ·

In This Chapter

▶ Deciding how to manage the property

▶ Understanding how to fill vacancies

▶ Dealing with leases, contracts and money collection

▶ Getting on with tenants

▶ Staying on the right side of the law

· ·

*B*y the time you settle on buying a rental property, you've probably already put in dozens, perhaps hundreds, of hours. Now, however, the real work begins. First you need to decide whether to manage the property yourself or pay for professional management. Then, to maximise the value of your investment, you've got to attract and retain excellent tenants, stay on top of government regulations, keep your eyes open for ways to cost-effectively improve your property, and handle contracts and money flowing in and going out. You also need to understand the requirements of your tenants and act fairly, both to them and in the eyes of the law.

Managing Yourself or Hiring Help?

A property owner is always required to make the major decisions over such things as expenditure on capital works and other major maintenance issues. But whoever manages your rental property — you or an agent you hire — needs to take responsibility for the ongoing management issues. These include marketing, tenant selection, rent collection, advertising and maintenance.

Ignorance is no excuse

If you're buying your first investment property, you probably don't have a lot of recent experience with rental properties. In fact, your only first-hand knowledge may be as a tenant years ago. You need to know many, many laws and regulations. And ignorance of the law is no excuse when you need to front a tenancy tribunal (which in many states tends to have a bias towards tenants over landlords).

You need to draw on varied sources of information if you're intending to manage your own property portfolio — the sort of information you need is covered throughout this chapter. However, we don't recommend that first-time landlords manage their own property. The cost of having a manager run your residential investment property is usually about 5.5 to 8.8 per cent, including GST, of your rent plus some additional charges. That is, if your property rents for $1,500 a month, the cost is approximately $120 a month (if the fee is 8 per cent). The fee is also a tax deduction.

The argument against managing your own *single* investment property is this: You need to know the same number of laws whether you own one investment property or ten. If you own one property, managing it yourself saves you about $120 a month. If you own ten properties, doing it yourself may then save you $1,200 a month. Managing your own properties may make more sense when you have more than a few to manage, as long as you have the time to devote to the task.

If you're intending to fill the management position yourself, you have to possess some basic skills. Although you don't need a degree or a lot of experience to get started, adopting a trial-and-error method is potentially dangerous. If you decide to manage the property yourself, make sure you do plenty of reading — on the laws themselves that affect tenancy in your state, as well as others' experience of them.

Assessing your skills as a property manager

Use the following questions to examine your own personality and skills to see if you're cut out to be your own property manager:

- ✓ **Are you a people person?** Serving as a landlord is largely about managing people. You must enjoy people and solving problems — while often being unappreciated yourself.

- ✓ **Do you have the temperament to handle problems?** Responding to complaints and service requests in a positive and rational manner is key.

- ✓ **Can you tackle basic accounting tasks?** Are you comfortable with numbers and meticulous with paperwork?

- ✓ **Do you have maintenance and repair abilities?** Being able to work effectively and efficiently with your hands goes a long way, because hiring contractors to cover all of your odd-job requirements can be costly.

- ✓ **Are you willing to work and take phone calls in the evenings and on weekends?** Who needs a weekend, right? Sadly, that's when things tend to blow up, break down and fall over.

- ✓ **Do you have sales and negotiation skills?** You need to sell the space.

- ✓ **Are you willing to commit the time and effort?** All these important tasks take time, and others — such as determining the right rent and becoming familiar with property-management laws — take even more time.

If you're impatient or easily manipulated, you aren't suited to being a property manager. You need to convey a professional demeanour to your tenants. They must see you as someone who is going to take responsibility for the condition of the property. You must also insist that tenants live up to their part of the bargain, pay their rent regularly, and refrain from causing unreasonable damage to your property.

A rental property manager must be fair, firm and friendly to all rental prospects and tenants. You need to treat everyone impartially and remain patient and calm under stress. You must be determined and unemotional in enforcing rent collection, as well as your policies and rules. And you must maintain a positive attitude through it all. Not as simple as it looks, is it?

When you manage a rental property, you don't have to deal with just your current tenants. You also have to interact with potential renters, tradespeople, suppliers, neighbours and government employees. People, not the property, create most rental-management problems. Be prepared to be flexible and learn from your property-management experiences. The really good property managers may have credentials, but they have also graduated from the school of hard knocks. Practice makes perfect.

Hiring professional management

Most suburban real estate agencies have a rental property management arm. Agents take on the responsibility for all ongoing operations of the property (or as much or as little as you're prepared to cede to them). The right agent can make a big difference in the cash flow your rental property generates by finding good replacement tenants quickly or making sure maintenance is done quickly and efficiently. (Agents usually have a list of qualified contractors who charge a standard fee for their agency's clients.) Find property managers familiar with your kind of investment property. With a little research, you can find the right fit for your property.

A poor management company cuts into your profits, not only with its fees, but also by providing improper maintenance and leasing to poor-quality tenants who run your property into the ground.

Researching local agents

Visit the office of agents working in the local area and spend time interviewing the specific agent who'll have hands-on management of your property. Make a few extra phone calls to check references and don't sign a management contract until you feel confident the company you hire has a sound track record. You need to call a few clients the agent has managed for. But that's not enough. Find out how long they've been a rental agent and how many properties they're looking after.

Rental property management companies have a notoriously high turnover. You may well find that, even if you like the rental management company, you're dealing with a different staff member each 6 to 12 months (it's happened to Bruce too regularly). This may, or may not, be an issue for tenants, who aren't necessarily long term. It's more likely to be an issue for you. Sadly, good, long-term, rental property managers can be a little hard to find. If you're not happy with what your manager is doing, you need to be prepared to sack him.

 Make sure the agency you hire manages sufficient properties in the area so that the agency is sought out by tenants. They don't need to be the biggest, but tenants tend to learn quickly which agencies have the largest number of properties in an area and gravitate to them. Although the largest rental agency in a suburb or town is no guarantee of the professionalism or good service of the agents working there, it does suggest that interested parties (landlords and tenants) believe that agency is where the traffic lies — and, when you've got an empty property, traffic is probably the most important element in getting your property tenanted again. Also be aware that running a rental management agency is a volume business and many real estate agencies only run rental businesses with the aim that the thin margins will possibly be made up later by obtaining the listing to sell the property.

Be sure to investigate these issues:

- ✔ **Licences:** Make sure the agency has the appropriate state-based licences to run rental properties.

- ✔ **Credentials:** Also examine the property managers' credentials — make sure they're members of their state real estate institute. Check the Real Estate Institute of Australia website (www.reia.com.au) for links to the state bodies.

- ✔ **Insurance:** The company should carry professional indemnity and public liability insurances. The management company is your agent and will be collecting your rents and security bonds, so you want to be sure it's protected against rogue employees.

In most management contracts, an *emergency clause* gives agencies the ability and right to perform emergency repairs without advance approval from the owner (usually up to a certain limit). This emergency clause allows the agent to take care of unexpected problems. The dollar limit should be commensurate with the type and size of the property. Most residential properties should have a limit of $1,000, although commercial properties and larger residential properties may need higher limits.

When you're in the early stages of working with a new agent, make sure you closely monitor the property's expenses. Even though the property manager may have the legal right to use funds up to a certain amount, she should always keep you informed.

Agency fees and charges

Typically in Australia, management companies receive a percentage of the collected income for managing a property. Usually, the larger the rental property, the lower the management fee percentage. Management fees for houses and apartments run between 5.5 and 8.8 per cent and are occasionally higher. Fees for commercial properties have a similar scale.

Additional fees for leasing a vacant property are often justified, because the most time-intensive portion of property management is tenant turnover. When one tenant leaves, the rental property or the commercial, industrial or retail suite must be made rent-ready; then the property manager must show the property and screen the tenants. Additional leasing charges for residential rentals can vary but are usually in the vicinity of one to two weeks' rent. Leasing commissions for commercial, industrial or retail properties are usually a percentage of the gross rent, with a declining scale — the longer the lease, the lower the percentage in later years.

DIY property management

Many first-time property investors do all the work themselves — painting, cleaning, making repairs, collecting rent, paying bills and showing the rental. However, after a while, most investors delegate jobs they don't enjoy or aren't suited to. Some new owners, of course, do just fine managing their own rental properties. But others discover first-hand that on-the-job management training can backfire in a costly way.

If you have the right traits for managing property, and the time, and live close to your property, you may consider doing it yourself. Among the advantages of self-management are the savings you can make in these areas:

   ✔ **Monthly property-management fees:** Property managers' fees aren't insignificant, so a potential advantage for the do-it-yourself approach is that you can save yourself money. However, you must examine the bigger picture of the value of your time and realistically assess how much of your time property management will take up.

> ✔ **Maintenance costs:** By keeping direct control of the management, you decide who does the repair work and mows the lawn. If you're qualified and have the time, doing your own maintenance or gardening is usually a good idea. Develop a list of reliable tradespeople who are licensed, do good work and charge fairly. And, when you need to find a new painter, gardener or carpenter, get recommendations from other contractors — in a local area they often see each other about and know who's doing good work and who should be avoided.

What's your time worth? Some owners who self-manage can tell you exactly how much money they 'saved' by not hiring an agent, but the factor they overlook is the value of their own time in dealing with management issues.

If you earn your living regularly from something other than managing rentals, managing your investment property may not be worth your valuable time. If you're a higher income, full-time professional, rushing off on weekdays to handle some minor crisis at your rental property isn't only impractical; it could be downright damaging to your career.

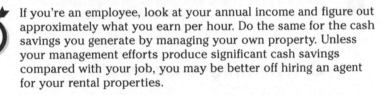

If you're an employee, look at your annual income and figure out approximately what you earn per hour. Do the same for the cash savings you generate by managing your own property. Unless your management efforts produce significant cash savings compared with your job, you may be better off hiring an agent for your rental properties.

The same guidelines hold true if you're an independent business owner or self-employed. Your schedule may be more flexible than that of a nine-to-five employee. But, if you're earning $80 an hour, devoting hours of your productive work time to managing rentals, which may amount to cash savings of only $35 an hour, doesn't make sense.

Renting Vacant Properties

Vacant properties don't generate rental income, so fill your vacancies with good, stable, rent-paying tenants quickly. Verifying information on prospective tenants' rental applications takes a while, but is time well spent. Relying on your instincts will largely be inaccurate, arbitrary and potentially illegal (particularly if it leads to discrimination).

Establishing tenant-selection criteria

In order to increase your chances of finding a long-term, stable tenant, your tenant-selection criteria and screening process should be clear, systematic and objective. Determine your minimum qualifications and adhere to them, applying them *consistently* and *fairly* to *all* rental applicants. You need to be aware of federal and state discrimination laws when determining who you'll let your property to.

Setting up a systematic screening process is particularly critical if you own only one or two properties. Deadbeat tenants who go from property to property causing damage and not paying rent are experienced and shrewd. They know novice property owners are more likely to be fooled and that professional agents have screening procedures to verify every single item on their applications. If certain items don't check out, professional managers don't just trust their feelings on the prospective tenant.

More than 90 per cent of your residential rental applicants will be good tenants, pay their rent on time, take good care of their homes, and treat you and their neighbours with respect. You just need to carefully guard against those few bad apples; don't hesitate to deny prospects who can't meet your standards.

Determining lease length

The *lease* or *rental agreement* is the legal document that specifies the terms and conditions of the contract that's supposed to bind the property owner and the tenant, although tenancy tribunals are increasingly refusing to punish tenants who walk out on leases. A lease is a contract between the owner of the property and the tenant for the possession and use of the property in exchange for the payment of rent for either residential or commercial property for a specific term:

 ✔ **Residential tenants:** No minimum or maximum term is set, but most residential leases are initially signed for one year (potentially six months). Landlords can offer a further set period at the end of the initial agreement but, often, the rent reverts to a month-to-month lease. Renters in this situation often stay on for many years, and landlords usually keep rent increases to a minimum in order to keep a good tenant on.

✔ **Commercial tenants:** Commercial, industrial and retail investment property owners almost always use long-term leases. Fixed-term contracts obligate you and the tenant for a set period; some owners like the commitment required from the tenant and tenants have certainty to assist the development of their business. With such a lease, renegotiating aspects of the lease — including rents and tenancy length — can't be done until the lease expires, unless both parties agree, or the tenant doesn't pay the rent or violates another term of the lease.

Setting the rent

Setting the rent is about walking a fine line. If you set your rent too high, you won't get tenants. No tenant equals trouble with the mortgage. And, if you set your rent too low, your income will suffer. Essentially, rents are set by market forces — supply and demand. If many properties are available for rent, tenants can be choosey. If a property shortage exists, landlords are in the box seat.

The best way to find out what your property's worth on the rental market is to either ask local agents or do the legwork yourself and visit six to 12 properties similar to yours in the area.

Setting the rent is particularly critical if you own a house or apartment or a small commercial property, because the rent loss from an extended vacancy or one bad tenant can seriously jeopardise your investment. Be conservative in setting your rents to attract good long-term tenants who pay on time. Using a conservative budget for your property that anticipates a slightly lower rent and at least two weeks' vacancy each year also helps to avoid nasty surprises.

Setting your rent properly should be an independent decision based on current market conditions. The realities of the market will put limits on what rent you can reasonably charge for your property.

Evaluating the rental rates being charged for similar properties in comparable locations is a great way to gather information before setting your own rent. Make minor adjustments in your rent because of variations in the location, age, size and features of the properties you're comparing.

For example, if you own a residential investment property and one of your competitors has an available rental nearly identical to yours, your rent should be slightly higher if you also have air conditioning. Of course, make a reduction for aspects of your rental property that aren't as desirable.

Adding value through renovations and upgrades

For residential properties, almost every rental has the potential for renovation or upgrades. Often, upgrades allow you to create the real value in rental properties: When you have a dated property, a renovation can allow the rent to be increased. Pay particular attention to items that are quick, easy and inexpensive to replace but can really improve the overall look, such as cupboard doors and handles, a new letterbox and basic light fittings.

If you have an older investment property, renovating or making tenant improvements may be more difficult due to some of the hazardous materials used in the building's original construction. Asbestos and lead-based paint were commonly used in many properties (prior to the early 1980s for asbestos and about 1970 for lead paint), and these materials can be quite costly to remove. Often, you're better off just leaving them in place, as long as they haven't been disturbed. Consult with experts in these issues before doing any work.

Again, if your chosen investment properties are residential, keep in mind what features and strengths your prospective tenants will find in competitive rentals. For example, if most of your competition offers dishwashers but your property doesn't have one, you may want to install a dishwasher so you remain competitive.

Enhancing external appearances

Make sure that your prospective tenants' first impressions of your residential or commercial rental property are positive, because, if they aren't, they'll most likely never take the time to see the interior. Start at the street and carefully critique your property as if you were entering a contest for the best-looking property in your area. Better still, get a friend to come past to cast a fresh eye over the property, as your familiarity with the property may mean you miss some of its faults.

To attract tenants who'll treat your property properly and stay for a long time, be sure that the grounds and exterior areas are sparkling clean and the landscaping is well maintained. Renovating the grounds by removing rubbish and weeds is an inexpensive task.

Make sure the entry is clean, well kept and well lit. The entry door should be cleaned or freshly painted. Buy a new welcome mat. Remove or replace a broken screen door.

Improving what's inside

The most qualified renters always have choices. You're in competition for these tenants and you need to ensure that your rental property stands out. The positive first impression of your rental property's exterior won't matter if the interior is poorly maintained.

Don't show your rental property until it's completely ready. Although you may lose a couple of potential showing days by taking the time to get everything ready, you'll benefit in the long run with a more conscientious tenant. Here's a list of things to check:

- ✔ All plumbing and appliances are operating properly.

- ✔ Counters, cabinets, doors, mouldings, thresholds and metal strips are clean and fully operational, presenting no hazards.

- ✔ Cupboards and storage areas, cupboard doors, rods, hooks, shelves and lights are in good order, and floors and walls are clean.

- ✔ Floor coverings are clean and in good condition.

- ✔ Heating and air conditioning are operational. Be sure the thermostat, filters, vents and registers are all in working order.

- ✔ Locks have been changed (although sometimes it may be unnecessary, you should always consider changing locks) and are operational. Pay attention to all latches and catches, doorknobs and pulls, doorstops and sliding doors.

- ✔ Paint and/or wall coverings provide proper coverage, without holes, cuts, scratches or nails.

- ✔ Patios, balconies and entries are clean and the railings secure.

✔ Smoke detectors, all lighting and electrical outlets, including circuit-breakers or safety switches, are working properly.

✔ The toilet, tub, shower, sink, mirrors and cabinets are thoroughly cleaned. If your budget allows or it's required, consider re-enamelling an old bathtub, replacing aged mirrors and installing a dual-flush cistern.

✔ Windows, window locks, screens and window coverings are clean, secure and operating properly.

Using contractors

Particular maintenance and improvements are best handled by qualified, licensed tradespeople. For example, doing your own pest extermination, dealing with hazardous chemicals or attempting to recharge the coolant in an air conditioning unit yourself would be unwise, as would doing your own electrical and plumbing jobs.

Every day your residential rental property sits vacant is costing you income that you can never recover. Painting your own rental may take you six days working in the evenings and weekends to complete. If the rental market is strong and the daily rental rate is $70 per day, you're actually losing money if you could've had the property professionally touched up in one day for $400 in labour (not including materials), given the loss in rental income for the six days it took you to complete the job is $420 — and you've had to soak up your own valuable holidays or down time to do the work.

Regardless of how much work you choose to handle yourself, have on hand a list of competent and competitively priced service companies and suppliers for those times when you need a quick response. Also ensure contractors have the proper insurance in place before you allow them to commence work on your property.

Advertising for tenants

Advertising is how you let people know that you have a vacant rental property available. Money intelligently spent on advertising is money well spent. When done poorly, advertising can be another black hole for your precious resources.

Determine the most desirable features of your rental property for your target market. You can also ask people who look at your property — whether or not they agree to rent — what aspects of your property they found of interest. Incorporate these selling points into your marketing efforts.

The best advertisement for your rental property is street appeal — the exterior appearance. Properties that have well-kept grounds with green grass, trimmed shrubs, beautiful flowers and fresh paint are much more appealing to your rental prospects. A well-maintained property often attracts a tenant who'll pay more rent and treat your rental property with care.

These days, the vast majority of potential tenants first see the property they end up renting on the internet. Although local newspapers are still useful, ignoring renters who may surf the Net trying to find their next abode is foolish.

One of the most time-consuming aspects of owning and managing rental property is the time spent filling vacancies. Real estate investors with commercial properties use professional leasing agents. Although most residential property investors also use real estate agents to have their place leased initially, those who have the inclination to take on the management individually should be aware that it can be a huge time trap.

Efficiently scheduling showings

The most efficient approach to showing your residential rental is to hold an 'open for inspection', which enables you to show your property to several interested rental prospects within half an hour or an hour. Select one or two 30-minute periods for your open house that are convenient for you and most working people (preferably during daylight hours). Combining a weekday early evening open house with one on the weekend enables virtually all prospects to fit the rental showing into their busy schedules.

Often a newspaper ad simply indicating the time of your 'open for inspection' is sufficient. If the place appeals and the advertised time is both short enough to create a sense of interest from those coming and going and long enough to allow those visiting properties all over town to see your property, you may find that an hour (or two one-hour stints) is long enough to get a couple of qualified applicants.

If you're trying to lease a property in a depressed rental market, or if you find you need to fill a vacancy during the holidays, you may not be able to generate enough interest from an open house to get a sense of urgency among multiple prospects. If you have to schedule individual appointments, keep these points in mind:

✔ **Be prepared to show your property at night and on weekends for short, but reasonable, time frames, when most of your prospects are available.**

✔ **If you've made appointments with individuals, call to verify the rental showing before making a special trip to the property.** By calling, you're also reassuring the prospect that you're going to be there and aren't going to be delayed. Exchanging mobile numbers can be helpful here.

Showing vacant versus occupied rentals

When showing a vacant residential rental, be a tour guide but don't be too controlling. Allow the prospects to view the rental in the manner that suits them. Some prospects go right to a certain room. If the prospects hesitate or are reluctant to tour on their own, casually guide them.

Most properties are typically shown vacant, although you may be able to obtain the cooperation of a vacating tenant to show prospects through the property while occupied. Because commercial tenants almost always require some specialised tenant improvements, working off drawings of the space rather than conducting a physical tour can be more useful. If you do show an occupied commercial space, just be sure not to disrupt the current tenant's business activities.

If the current residential tenants are at the end of their lease or have given notice to vacate, the owner is usually allowed to enter the property to show prospective new tenants. You must comply with state laws that require you to give tenants advance written notice of entry prior to showing the rental.

Cooperate with the current tenants when scheduling mutually convenient times to show the rental — and respect their privacy by avoiding excessive intrusions. Although the current tenant may be legally required to allow you and your prospects to enter the rental property for a showing, she doesn't have to make any efforts to ensure that the property is clean and neat.

Showing a vacant rental is usually much easier, but touring your prospects through an occupied rental property does have some advantages, particularly if your current tenants are friendly, cooperative and are leaving for understandable reasons (such as having bought a house or needing more room for a larger family). The rental prospects may want to ask the current tenant questions about their living experience at your property.

If your current residential tenant is being evicted, isn't leaving on good terms or has an antagonistic attitude for any reason, don't show the rental until the property is vacated. Also consider this strategy if your current tenants haven't taken care of the rental property or if their lifestyle or furnishings may be objectionable to some rental prospects. Also bear in mind that, sometimes, showing a property while the current tenants are in the throes of moving can invite your prospective tenants into a nightmare of boxes, half-packed clothes and uncleaned walls and carpets. Use your judgement.

Communicating with prospective tenants

Tenants want to feel they can communicate with you if a problem arises. They also appreciate someone showing an interest in their lives. By showing an interest, you set yourself apart from other property managers. Some prospects will take a rental property that isn't exactly what they're looking for if they have a positive feeling about the property owner.

Your goal at the end of the showing is to receive a commitment to rent from the prospect by having him complete your rental application. But don't forget that you still need to thoroughly screen the prospect and confirm that he meets your rental criteria before you sign a lease or rental agreement.

Taking and verifying applications

Offer every interested prospect the opportunity to complete an application. Information provided on the application enables you to begin the screening process and select the best tenant for your rental property.

Prior to accepting the rental application, carefully review the entire form to make sure each prospective tenant has legibly provided all requested information. Perhaps offer prospects an option to fill in the form online, print it off and sign it before sending it in. Pay particular attention to all names and addresses, employment information, driver's licence numbers and emergency contacts. Make sure that the prospect has signed the rental application authorising you to verify the provided information and to run a credit report. Ask each prospective tenant to show you her current driver's licence or other photo ID so that you can confirm her correct name and current address. Write down or photocopy the details of photo ID for your records.

If a rental prospect dithers through the process, delays returning phone calls or insists on additional time, cutting your losses and moving on to the next prospect may be best.

Ask about any discrepancies between the application and the ID provided. Even if the explanation seems reasonable, be sure to write down the new information.

Rental history

When you first contact the rental applicant's current agent or landlord, listen to his initial reaction and let him tell you about the applicant. Some agents or landlords welcome the opportunity to give you information about your rental applicant, but others may be

- ✔ **Dishonest:** An agent or landlord may be upset with the tenant for leaving his property, or unwilling to say anything bad about a problem tenant so that he can get the tenant out of his property and into yours.

- ✔ **Unforthcoming:** Some agents or landlords may hold back information because they're concerned they'll cop liability if they provide any negative or subjective information.

When a current or prior agent or landlord isn't overly cooperative, try to gain her confidence by providing her with some information about yourself and your rental property. If you're still unable to build rapport, try to get her to at least answer the most important question of all: 'Would you rent to this applicant again?' She can simply give you a 'yes' or a 'no' without any details. Of course, silence can also tell you everything you need to know.

Written references are almost worthless without having them thoroughly backed up verbally by the author.

Employment and income

Independently verify the company information and phone number the applicant puts on his application if you have any doubts about its authenticity. Get the applicant's permission to speak to one of his superiors, and specifically to discuss the sensitive issues of income and stability of employment. Be prepared to send letters requesting the information and include a self-addressed, stamped envelope, though email may suffice. Be sure to tell your rental prospect that you may have a delay in providing him with the results. Also, request recent payslips from the rental prospect. For prospective commercial tenants, a copy of the most recent tax return, or verified letter from their accountant, could be suitable.

Credit history

In Australia, privacy laws mean that in order to obtain a credit report on an applicant, you need the applicant's signed permission to check the various credit databases. A credit report shows all current and previous credit cards and loans, credit repayment issues, plus all public record entries such as bankruptcy and judgement. You can figure out whether an applicant has been late or delinquent in paying her rent or other living expenses. The two major credit-reporting agencies in Australia are Dun & Bradstreet (www.checkyourcredit.com.au) and Veda Advantage (www.mycreditfile.com.au).

 Carefully compare the addresses contained on the credit report with the information provided on the rental application. If you find an inconsistency, ask the rental prospect for an explanation. He may have a logical reason. Information obtained in credit reports must be kept strictly confidential.

Notifying applicants of your decision

Be sure to notify the successful applicant promptly when you make your decision. You may want to request a part-payment — a week's rent is common — as a holding deposit at this point. (Sometimes this is requested from an applicant who's likely to be successful but is awaiting a final reference check, for instance, with the deposit refunded if the application fails the final check.) You could also notify any applicants who've failed to meet the criteria, because you won't be offering the property to them in any case.

 Don't notify the other qualified applicants that you've already rented out the property until all legal documents have been signed and all funds due upon move-in have been collected in full. This way, if your first-choice tenant can't take the property or was successful elsewhere, you haven't sent other qualified tenants out to continue their own searches.

Signing Leases and Collecting Money

Tenants and property owners alike are usually aware of all the legal paperwork involved in renting a property. And, although sifting through all that legalese isn't fun for anyone, it *is* important. Rental property owners and tenants each have specific legal rights and responsibilities that are outlined in these documents, and being aware of what you're agreeing to — and being sure your tenants know what they're agreeing to — is crucial.

Reviewing and signing documents

After you approve your selected tenant, you should have her sign the rental agreement as soon as is practical.

Be sure that your tenant understands that when she signs your rental agreement she's entering into a contract that has significant rights and responsibilities for both parties. Be sure to have all adult occupants review and sign *all documents* — including any lease or rental agreement addendums — before taking possession of the rental property. Never enter oral agreements with tenants — it opens the door to much potential confusion.

Collecting the money

Be sure to collect the first month's rent (or two weeks' rent in some states and territories) and the bond (usually four weeks' or one month's rent) *before* you give the tenants the keys. Payment for rent may be in the form of cash, a bank cheque or, preferably, electronic transfer. If you accept a personal cheque, don't hand over the keys until the cheque has cleared. Provide receipts for all payments. And make sure that you and the tenant are perfectly clear how rent will be paid for the remainder of the lease. Your preference should be for electronic transfer, which is most efficient for all concerned.

The *rental*, or *security*, *bond* is a deposit from the tenant on the property as a possible part-payment against the cost of potential damage and non-payment of rent. Landlords are not allowed to physically hold rental bonds paid by tenants in Australia. The bond, which is usually limited to one month's rent for residential properties, is required to be made out to a government-run organisation. These agencies act as a trust and hold the bond on behalf of the landlord and tenant in case of dispute at the end of the tenancy. If a dispute arises, getting access to the money usually requires an application to a state tenancy tribunal.

Inspecting the property with your tenant

When properly completed, the inspection form clearly documents the condition of the rental property upon move-in by the tenants and serves as a baseline for the entire tenancy. If the tenant withholds rent or tries to break the lease claiming the property needs substantial repairs, you may need to be able to prove the condition of the rental upon move-in. When the tenants move out, you'll be able to clearly note the items that have been damaged or haven't been left clean by the vacating tenants.

Complete the inspection form *with the tenants* prior to or at the time of move-in. Walk through the premises with the tenants and agree that all items are clean and undamaged, or note any pre-existing damage, *before* they move in. Note the condition of the floor coverings — one of the most common areas of dispute upon departure. Although tenants shouldn't be charged for ordinary wear and tear, if they destroy the carpet, they should pay for the damage. Most lease documents now stipulate that a tenant must steam-clean carpets before they hand in the keys at the end of the tenancy. Taking photos of the property to refresh the tenant's (or your own) memory at the end of the tenancy, or to show in court, can be helpful.

Working with Existing Tenants

Although most residential investment property in Australia is sold as 'vacant at possession', occasionally the rental property you've recently acquired has tenants already living there. Tenants are typically full of apprehension when the ownership of the property they're renting is changing, so beginning your relationship with your tenants on a positive note is extremely important.

Meeting tenants and inspecting the property

When you first acquire a tenanted residential rental property, contact the tenants and reassure them you intend to treat them with respect. Deal with tenants' questions honestly and directly. The most common concerns usually include the following:

- ✔ Potential for a rent increase

- ✔ Proper maintenance or condition of their rental property

- ✔ Continuation of certain policies, such as allowing pets

Just as you're evaluating your tenant, your tenant is evaluating you during these initial contacts. Failing to be open and honest can result in a loss of credibility should you later implement changes that you didn't acknowledge up-front. And don't make any promises that you won't keep.

If you're investing in commercial investment properties, you should also meet with your tenants and listen to their concerns about the property. Although they typically aren't as concerned about sudden rent increases (because they're likely on a long-term lease), they are interested in hearing about your plans to maintain and upgrade the property or make any other improvements that may aid their business. Also, it's never too soon to begin courting your commercial tenants for a lease renewal.

Provide your tenants with a letter of introduction during this brief in-person meeting. This letter provides your tenant with your contact information, explains your rent-collection policies and the proper procedures for requesting maintenance.

Although you've most likely viewed the interior of the property prior to purchase or settlement, walking through again with the tenant, now that you're the owner, can be helpful. Pay special attention to the proper use of the space, particularly for commercial properties, where illegal activities such as the use or storage of hazardous materials could be a serious liability issue.

Entering into a new rental agreement

Although you may want to make some changes to the lease terms or policies when you acquire an occupied rental property, your legal and business relationship is already established by whatever agreement the tenants had with the former owner. Therefore, you need to wait until the expiration of the lease to change the terms — or provide the tenant with proper written notice of proposed changes as required by law.

New owners may attempt to convert existing tenants to their own lease or rental agreement as soon as possible. Keep the following in mind:

- ✔ **Residential tenancies:** Implementing your own rental agreement as soon as legally allowed is relatively easy and can be done upon the expiration of the lease and normally upon 60 days' written notice if the tenant is on a month-to-month rental agreement. However, most rental agreements in Australia are fairly standard and rarely need to be significantly changed.

- ✔ **Commercial properties:** The existing leases are valid and binding until their expiration, so you must wait to implement new leases until tenant lease renewal or turnover.

Increasing rents

When you acquire an investment property, part of your research is to establish the fair market rental value of your new property. If the tenant's current rent is below market value and he's on a month-to-month rental agreement, one of your toughest jobs is how to implement rent increases. As the new owner, you're likely to have much higher mortgage payments and expenses to make necessary repairs and upgrades to the property than the last owner did. No tenant wants a rent increase, so you'll be able to do little to appease him.

The majority of tenants will reluctantly accept a rent increase as long as the rent isn't raised beyond the current market rent for a comparable place in the area and you're willing to make needed repairs or upgrades to their rental property or suites.

Avoiding Discrimination Complaints

Discriminating against tenants based on religion, sex, nationality, age, marital status or disability is illegal. Stiff penalties can be awarded against landlords who discriminate. Problems often arise because property owners are unaware that their policies or practices are discriminatory. Discrimination laws also impact on your advertising, tenant-screening and selection process.

Being fair to families and children

All residential rental properties must be offered to all applicants, including those with children. However, because non-residential properties are less regulated, some commercial property owners may be within their legal rights to use their business judgement to refuse or discourage an applicant with plans to use the leased space as, for example, a day-care facility or other business that caters for children.

As a residential rental property owner, you should welcome renters with children. Families tend to be more stable and they look for safe, low-crime and drug-free environments in which to raise their kids. Along with responsible pet owners, who also have difficulty finding suitable rental properties, families with children can be excellent long-term renters. And, typically, the longer your tenants stay, the better your cash flow.

Dealing with tenants with disabilities

Federal and state laws stipulate that communities should be blind to (as in not notice or discriminate against) people's disabilities, including when it comes to financial matters. In Australia, not all houses, units or commercial properties are required to be accessible to people with disabilities. But some properties will naturally be more suitable to a tenant with a disability.

Governments and the courts are not in the practice of forcing private landlords with single houses to spend thousands of dollars putting in ramps and widening doorways to potentially cover tenants with disabilities. But, if you have a multi-unit property, you may be required to

✔ Make reasonable accommodations at your expense for
tenants with disabilities, so they can enjoy the rental
property on an equal basis.

✔ Make reasonable adjustments to the rules, procedures
or services, upon request. A common example would be
providing a wider and more convenient parking space, if
practical.

✔ Allow tenants with a disability the right to modify their
living space at their own expense, as long as

• The modifications only extend to what is necessary to
make the space safe and comfortable.

• The tenant agrees to restore the property to its original
condition upon vacating the property (when it's
reasonably likely that the tenant *will* vacate).

• The tenant obtains your prior approval and ensures that
the work is done in a professional manner, including
obtaining any necessary government approvals
or permits.

Animals that assist tenants with daily life activities (such as
guide dogs) must be allowed in all rental properties, regardless
of any no-pet policies.

Dealing with tenants and pets

Tenants and their pets are an issue that landlords come up
against from time to time. Some tenants will be up-front about
owning a pet when they seek to rent a property. Others may
deliberately fail to disclose that they have pets when they fill out
an application form. Some tenants acquire pets only after they
move into the property.

Most standard leases contain a condition stating the tenants
aren't allowed to have pets without written permission — a
'no-pets' clause. The majority of tenants understand that
landlords don't want pets and will comply. But occasionally you
may have to get tough about it. Pets can cause serious damage.
Carpets are an obvious danger, but cats and dogs may also
scratch furnishings, rip apart gardens, kill grass and, of course,
poop everywhere.

Some landlords are pet lovers and won't be concerned about tenants with pets — if that's the case, you might even advertise as being a pet-friendly landlord. You're bound to be inundated with potential tenants.

Tenancy tribunals have been known to back landlords when they evict tenants who lied about having pets in the first place or who refuse to get rid of pets acquired after moving in. But the issue isn't clear-cut, so be prepared to defend yourself in tribunal or a court if you want to evict a tenant.

Chapter 9

Building a Portfolio

'The journey of 10,000 miles starts with a single step.' This old proverb can be easily adapted to explain the most important concept in the world of investment. That is, if you have a certain dream or ambition — to be that successful businessperson, self-made investment millionaire or property tycoon — you don't just magically become that person. You have to make a start, or *take that first step*.

Property portfolios don't just appear (unless your property-portfolio-owning parents died and left you the lot). The most successful real estate investors inevitably start with a single property. How they move from there to being the owners of a 'multimillion-dollar portfolio' is a well-worn path that has been followed by millions of people around the world. Investing in property isn't a step-by-step process that guarantees success, but offers enough common principles for those with commitment to follow.

Property investment isn't necessarily easy. And it requires years of patience and probably a bit of luck. Property prices can go through long periods of stagnation or even falling *real* prices (that is, after taking into account inflation), which removes the easiest way to having your properties create wealth — capital growth. During some cycles, rents can also refuse to nudge higher, which can dull returns and deny the cash funding for subsequent property purchases. Both of these regular cycles can knock the commitment out of people who are initially enthusiastic about building a portfolio before they've really tasted success.

Getting your mind around building a portfolio largely comes down to understanding a few basic principles — the laws of investment that are the building blocks upon which real property wealth is created. Once grasped, it will be an easier stretch to accept some of the realities of managing a property portfolio — being a landlord to many, diversifying your property holdings, maximising your tax position and owing a bank, potentially, a few million dollars — all of which we discuss in this chapter.

Using Property's Power Tools

The power of compounding returns and the power of leverage are the real secrets behind building a profitable real estate portfolio. They allow even those with relatively modest incomes to control multimillion-dollar portfolios. Along with knowing the basics of the property market itself, a deep understanding of how these two forces can be harnessed to build a portfolio is imperative.

Compounding returns

School maths classes taught you about the 'power of compounding interest'. If you put $100 into a bank account earning 10 per cent interest, at the end of a year, your $100 will be worth $110. That is, it will have grown by $10. If you leave that $110 in for another year at 10 per cent interest, it will be worth $121. In the second year it will have grown by $11, or $1 more than its growth in the first year. In the third year it will grow by $12.10; in the fifth year, by $14.64; in the tenth year, by $23.58.

Property investment can be an incredibly powerful investment tool because of the power of compounding. A $400,000 property that rises by a consistent 5 per cent each year will be worth

$420,000 at the end of the first year, $441,000 at the end of the second year, $510,000 at the end of year five and $651,000 at the end of the tenth year.

No property increases in price uniformly. In some years, prices may rise 20 or 25 per cent, while in others they may stay stable. Worse — and don't let seminar-based property spruikers fool you — prices can go backwards in real and in actual terms. But the theory of compounding is an important one for property investors, because it's the basis for the development of all portfolios.

Powering with leverage

Aside from the power of compounding (refer to the preceding section), an even more important concept behind property wealth is the power of leverage. Leverage, also known as gearing, is probably the pivotal reason that property is a favoured investment form for many of the world's most financially successful people.

In investment terms, *leverage* is simply another name for borrowing money to invest. Leveraging is about using OPM (other people's money) to buy property. Like all loans, you're renting OPM, the price of which is called 'interest'.

The fact is that few people buy property with their own cash (and many people invest in property using solely OPM). Most people buy their first property by saving up a deposit, and then borrowing the remaining necessary funds from a bank or other lender to purchase the property.

Almost all property is bought with some size of loan attached. Often, especially for property investors with substantial equity in other properties, the entire purchase price of the property, plus associated purchase costs, is borrowed (refer to Chapter 3 for information on how much to borrow).

Borrowing for property investment means you're taking higher risks. The concept of leverage applies to both rising and falling property values. If you're leveraged and prices fall, your financial position deteriorates faster than someone who doesn't have as much debt. Although investment debt is a proven wealth accumulator over long periods, you need to make sure you understand the risks on both the upside and the downside before borrowing large sums to invest.

Combining compound returns and leverage

The real attraction of property to those who've built, or are building, their own property portfolio is what happens when the two powerful forces of compound returns and leverage are put together over an extended period.

A $400,000 property that increases by 5 per cent in a year will be worth $420,000 at the end of that year. But what happens if the buyer who paid the $400,000 for the property in the first place put down only 10 per cent of the purchase price ($40,000) as her own money and borrowed the rest ($360,000)? At the end of a year, if her property has grown by 5 per cent, she will now have equity in the property of $60,000 ($420,000 less the $360,000 loan). Her initial $40,000 equity in the property has grown by 50 per cent in a year, to be worth $60,000. After two years, her ownership will have grown to $81,000 and at the end of year ten (assuming no loan principal has been paid off), her equity will have grown to approximately $291,000. Not a bad return in ten years on her initial $40,000 investment.

And what happens to an investor who owns a $2 million portfolio when a 5 per cent rise in values occurs in a year? Her portfolio rises in value by $100,000. However, if the investor had equity of $500,000 on her $2 million portfolio (and, therefore, had debt of around $1.5 million) and the portfolio rose by 5 per cent, the investor's $500,000 in equity grows to $600,000, or by 20 per cent.

Buying Your Second Investment Property

Putting the theory into action to build a property portfolio isn't as hard as it may sound. For a start, the good news is that by the time you're in a position to buy your second investment property, you've obviously already learned enough to buy your first — therefore, you don't need to relearn the basics of investment. Additionally, and somewhat inevitably, you'll have made a few mistakes along the way. And we're sure you'll have learned from those too.

Typically, buying your second investment property will occur after you've developed some equity in your home and your first investment property. (We don't include your home as an investment property for reasons explained in Chapter 2, but for many the second investment property will be the third property they buy.) For those without a home, the theory of moving from your first investment property to your second is the same as it is for those with a home. The purchase is usually made possible by using the equity already built from previous purchases to help cover the next purchase.

While the value of properties grows, the usual occurrence is that the debt either stays the same or perhaps even falls slowly (if you're paying principal and interest on one or more of your loans). Rising property values give you growing equity — and it's equity that will both bring you wealth from your property and give the bank the security it needs to be confident to lend you more money.

Here's a typical example of increasing equity: A couple bought their home ten years ago and, after spending six years paying down some of their home loan, they bought an investment property. The initial cost of their home was $250,000, which has now grown in value to $550,000 (after some renovations helped improve the property's value). They did their best to pay down the debt on their home in the first few years, but they still retain a debt of $80,000. The investment property they bought four years ago for $280,000 is now worth $340,000. Because they took out an interest-only loan on the investment property, the loan is still $297,000. They're considering buying another investment property valued at $360,000.

Current position:

Home value: $550,000

Home loan: $80,000

Investment property value: $340,000

Investment property loan: $297,000

Total loan-to-value ratio (LVR): 42.4 per cent

Second investment loan request:

Investment property value: $360,000

Investment property loan: $382,000

LVR of second investment property: 106.1 per cent (approx.)

Combined position (home and two investment properties):

Value of joint properties: $1,250,000

Value of joint loans: $759,000

LVR of all properties: 60.7 per cent

The investor couple now have two purely investment properties worth $700,000. However, including their home, they now have property assets worth $1.25 million (although the home is not an investment property, the equity it holds can be used to help fund property investments).

In most cases, assuming the couple have a reasonable income, a lender would usually be comfortable lending them the extra funds for their second investment property, assuming their financial circumstances haven't changed significantly since they bought their first investment property.

Now the couple have a debt of $759,000 — more than the value of their own home. Of that, they get to claim against their tax the interest paid on loans of $679,000.

Over time, rents themselves also rise. Apart from paying down the debt on your investment property (which many investors rightly choose not to do if they still have non-investment debt in their names, such as a home mortgage), rising rents should also help you turn negatively geared property into positively geared property, or help you pay down non-deductible personal debt.

Buying the Third, Fourth, Fifth and Beyond

Buying your second investment property is usually much less nerve-wracking than buying your first because you've had some experience. By the time you're in a position to buy your third investment property, the basic theory should be deeply ingrained and you'll have refined your own processes, including location search criteria (see 'Diversifying Your Portfolio' later in this chapter), property style and desired house traits. With that in mind, we take a look at buying that third property and then buying, say, a sixth property.

Property three

For the purposes of this example, we again assume that the investors' first property purchase was a home. Since then, they've bought two investment properties. We continue with the example couple from earlier in this chapter, but we're now three years later. By this time, their entire property-holding portfolio has increased by 5 per cent per annum.

REMEMBER

As the general price of properties rise, so does the value of the average property investment.

Current position:

Home value: $633,000

Investment properties value: $810,000

Value of all properties: $1,443,000

Home loan: $80,000

Investment property loans: $679,000

Total loans: $759,000

Total LVR: 52.5 per cent

Third investment loan request:

Investment property value: $410,000

Investment property loan: $435,000

LVR of new investment property: 106.1 per cent (approx.)

Combined position (home and three investment properties):

Value of all properties: $1,853,000

Value of all loans: $1,194,000

Total LVR: 64.4 per cent

The couple now have properties that, combined, are worth more than $1.85 million, with debts of nearly $1.2 million. Some people simply can't get their heads around this — the thought of owing a bank nearly $1.2 million wouldn't allow them to sleep properly at night. For them, property investment may be too difficult a step to take. But property investment and significant debt go hand in hand. And what usually occurs is that those who begin property investment learn to understand the nature of investment debt (see 'Understanding Good Debt versus Bad Debt' later in this chapter) and become comfortable with more and more debt over time.

But, if you want to see some serious debt, read on.

Property six

For the investors' sixth property, we've continued to assume growth of 5 per cent a year and that our investor couple have (after their second investment property, bought in year 10) bought an investment property every three years. To give the time line some perspective, 22 years have passed since they bought their home, 16 years since they bought their first investment property and 9 years since they bought investment property number three. They bought their fourth investment property 6 years ago and their fifth investment property 3 years ago.

If we assume that the couple bought their home when they were 30, they're now 52 years old. (They're probably near the height of their careers and have probably had a couple of children.) They've nearly paid off their home and have five investment properties.

Current position:

Combined property values: $4,131,000

Combined property loans: $2,201,000

Total LVR: 53.2 per cent

Sixth investment loan request:

Investment property value: $620,000

Investment property loan: $657,000

Total LVR of sixth investment property: 106 per cent (approx.)

Combined position (home and six investment properties):

Value of all properties: $4,751,000

Value of all loans: $2,858,000

Total LVR: 60.2 per cent

The investors now have a portfolio worth more than $4.75 million. Approaching five million dollars! If they stop right there, their property portfolio will be worth approximately more than $7 million by the time they turn 60, or $8.958 million by the time they're 65. That should be enough to retire on!

In these examples, we have assumed no repayment of debt, although rising rents and positive gearing would probably have allowed this to happen.

Even though this example is looking at a scenario that's probably 12 years from 2012 (assuming that the second investment property was purchased in 2012), the couple now has a clearly large debt by anyone's standards. Many will dismiss this concept as not being possible for them: 'There's no way a bank will lend me that much money!'

If you're thinking that, what you might be forgetting is that the investors don't just have their normal wages to help them meet the mortgage repayments. They also have tenants helping by paying rent (see 'Getting comfortable with big debt' later in this chapter) and the Tax Office will be helping with tax deductions and allowances for depreciation.

Growing Equity

Property investors tend to continue to hold on to their properties, meaning most wealth made from property continues to sit inside the property asset class, essentially for two reasons. The first is that property entry and exit fees are usually large (up to 6 per cent for entry and about 3 per cent to exit). The second reason is tax — the moment you sell a property (or, more accurately, when the beneficial ownership changes), capital gains tax (CGT) becomes payable and, therefore, a portion of your gains are handed back to the government.

To avoid the high entry and exit fees and capital gains tax, property investors don't buy and sell properties like some investors turn over their shares. If you have to make up to 6 per cent in entry costs and 3 per cent in exit costs, your property has to make at least 9 per cent before you make a cent of profit, plus the time cost of holding the investment. This fact is one of the reasons property is considered a long-term investment, particularly in Australia. (As a comparison, New Zealand has no stamp duty or capital gains tax. And, in the US, you can escape CGT by reinvesting the proceeds of your investment within a year.)

If you have a portfolio of properties, like the six-strong portfolio modelled earlier in this chapter, you could manage your holdings so that, when the time comes to sell, you have some choice over how much tax you pay.

Getting comfortable with big debt

If you're aiming to become a property mogul, you'd best get used to the idea of owing banks large sums of money. Direct property is an expensive asset class to buy into and it almost inevitably requires putting up some of your own equity and borrowing the rest from a lender.

If you own six properties, as in the example earlier in this chapter (refer to the section 'Property six') and you've made the most of tax laws to do so, you'll have large debt — nearly $2.9 million in the example we looked at. That's a difficult thing for many people to understand. Many experts believe in paying down the debt on a property as fast as possible to ensure that the investment becomes positively geared. They also argue that the size of the portfolio doesn't change that position. But, particularly in the early years of buying a property, paying down the debt often doesn't make sense (see the section 'Understanding Good Debt versus Bad Debt' later in this chapter).

Servicing a 'menagerie of mortgages'

Along with that property portfolio comes the menagerie of mortgages — an array of loans that will often be wildly different in size (and occasionally lenders), even if the beast is always the same (it's still the same old money).

How do you service six properties with nearly $2.9 million of debt (refer to the example in the section 'Property six' earlier in this chapter)? We wouldn't dare say 'easy'. But you don't have to come up with $217,500 a year (that's about 7.5 per cent, our preferred average rate for considering medium-term interest rates, of $2.9 million) yourself.

Negative gearing is (likely) here to stay

Every decade or so — usually when property prices are hitting new peaks and a chorus of concern is raised about whether young people will ever be able to buy their own property — comes the inevitable call for the abolition of negative-gearing tax breaks. The urgings usually come from individual federal politicians (who aren't speaking on behalf of their party) and state politicians (who have no power over federal tax law), perhaps even a few welfare groups who are keen to be seen to be doing or saying something about the plight of first-home buyers. Or, cynically, they're just trying to grab an easy headline.

The theory is that, if you remove the tax incentives for negative gearing, investors won't be as keen to invest in property. Many would sell out of their negatively geared investments, putting downward pressure on prices, allowing younger people to buy in — a logical argument.

The problem, not usually thought through by those proposing the abolition of tax breaks, is the *flow-on* effect of investors either selling property en masse, or refusing to invest in property.

What happens if investors aren't interested in property? Two things. First, lower demand means the price of property will fall (as is intended). And, although that may allow first-home buyers to enter the market, it will also *dramatically cut the wealth of those who've already bought their own houses*. Those people who've already bought their homes are voters too. And they're not going to be too happy with falling house prices.

Second (this point is what's usually forgotten), if investors aren't buying property to rent out, those who wish to rent have fewer places to live. If there's less supply of rental housing, those who still can't afford to buy, or don't want to buy, will have to pay higher rents.

This 'theory' went into practice in Australia in the mid-1980s, when the then Labor government removed negative-gearing provisions. What followed was falling house prices and aggressive rent increases. Within two years, negative-gearing tax breaks were reintroduced. (Arguably, if the law had stayed, the market would have eventually settled itself into some sort of equilibrium. But the backlash was so strong — by investors and tenants — that immediate action was taken.)

Negative gearing isn't necessarily permanently entrenched — but it will be a brave government that tries to remove it again.

First, you have tenants paying rent. In many cases, over the time you've taken to build the portfolio, the first few properties bought will have seen rent increases and they may now be individually positively geared. Second, depending on the type of property you've bought, you may have a fair amount of depreciation on the capital cost of the houses, providing significant tax deductions. Depreciation is a de facto form of income for a property investor, by way of a tax return for the depreciation in value of the bricks and mortar.

If rent and depreciation don't cover your costs, you have a third prong. The Tax Office gives you a portion of your losses back each year because of existing tax rules on negative gearing.

This combination of 'incomes' — rent, depreciation and negative-gearing tax returns — could possibly give an investor with a $2.9 million loan portfolio a neutrally or even positively geared investment portfolio.

Keeping an eye on leverage

The sorts of debts that are racked up in property portfolios are significant and should be constantly monitored. Your lender, or lenders, will monitor your debt level themselves anyway and won't lend you money if they perceive a big enough risk that you might 'fall over'. But, the more property investors get used to debt, the more debt they tend to be happy to take on. Getting used to the debt that comes with the first investment property is significantly harder than signing up for the debt that takes you from $2 million to $2.4 million.

What is more important is the level of leverage in your portfolio. Banks essentially issue their own warning when an investor's overall level of debt exceeds 80 per cent on assets by insisting on lenders' mortgage insurance (refer to Chapter 5) being paid. Say the value of your properties is $2 million. Some banks will let you borrow up to $1.6 million (80 per cent) without charging lenders' mortgage insurance (but this will depend on a number of other factors, including your personal income and rent-related income).

And, particularly since the GFC, banks have been pulling the reins on lending. They simply aren't prepared to lend to individuals to the same levels as they had before. And increased regulation has meant that they can't write the same loans that they used to previously, such as 'low-doc' and 'no-doc' loans.

Be sure to keep your own eye on your debt levels and what you're comfortable with. Keep a *constant* eye on what property prices are in your area to give you a good idea of what your property's worth. Also be aware of the debt you're carrying. Divide the debt by the total property value and multiply that by 100 to find your personal loan-to-value ratio (LVR). For example:

$$\text{Leverage (LVR)} = \frac{\$1.3 \text{ million}}{\$1.7 \text{ million}} \times 100 = 76.5\%$$

 Although occasionally going over 80 per cent LVR (and so incurring lenders' mortgage insurance) may be okay in the early stages of your property portfolio development, going over every time you invest in another property would be highly inadvisable. Indeed, this is generally no longer possible since the GFC has seen increased regulation on lenders and some fringe lending opportunities. Lenders' mortgage insurance is expensive (and a waste of money in that it covers your bank and not you).

Funding Several Properties

As your debt grows, you may want to consider a few other funding issues, including whether you want to put your other properties, including your home, at risk or not. On this point you need to consider the two different types of loans — recourse and non-recourse loans. (Refer to Chapter 4 for more on loan types.)

✔ **Recourse financing:** For these types of loans the bank will take other assets as security in determining the funding for the loan. If the borrower is prepared to put up other substantial assets (normally other property) as collateral for the loan, the bank will feel more comfortable about the debt and may charge a lower rate. Full recourse loans are the most common type of loan offered for personal property loans.

✔ **Non-recourse financing:** When the bank can't seek any other assets of a borrower to cover any shortfall, should the borrower be unable to repay the loan, the bank may offer non-recourse financing. These loans usually involve higher hurdles, not the least of which is usually a higher interest rate to cover the higher risk the bank is taking on. These types of loans are rare in Australia for personal property loans.

> ✔ **Limited recourse financing:** A legal requirement with loans made to self-managed superannuation funds (SMSFs), limited recourse loans mean the banks can generally only come after the asset that was used as security for the loan. In the case of SMSFs, lenders have then sought *director's guarantees* against loan defaults, which means directors have to repay loan shortfalls without resorting to the funds of the SMSF.

Understanding Good Debt versus Bad Debt

The concepts of 'good debt' and 'bad debt' need to be discussed here because of their importance to paying down debt when an investor has a lot of it. Bad debt is debt that you can't claim a tax deduction for. It's essentially for consumer goods and includes debt on credit cards, cars, holidays, home renovations and your own home. Good debt is debt that you can claim a tax deduction for, which is predominantly investment debt.

Why is there a difference? The cost of servicing $100 of interest on bad debt is $100. The cost of servicing $100 of interest on a good debt can be as little as $53.50, if you're on the top marginal tax rate, because of the tax-deductibility of investment debt.

 What does the concept of good debt versus bad debt mean for investors? It means that, if an investor has a mix of good and bad debt in her life, any spare money she has for debt reduction should be used to pay down her bad debt. Investors, particularly in their early years, often still owe money on their own home. That's the debt they should concentrate on reducing with spare capital. Because of the tax-deductibility of investment debt, no point exists in paying down investment debt while you still have bad debt — including for your own home — on your books.

Diversifying Your Portfolio

The concept of diversification is simple: If you have all your eggs in one basket and the person holding the basket lets go or stumbles, all of your eggs are going to smash. If you have several people holding your eggs in several baskets and one of these people drops a basket, you've still got a lot of other people (hopefully) safely holding your other eggs. (Refer to Chapter 2 for a discussion of diversification.)

Diversity of opinion on diversification

Not everyone agrees on the basic concept of investment diversification. Property investors have diverse opinions on diversifying property assets.

Some investors believe that owning property relatively near your own home can be sensible, because investors know their own market best. They can keep in contact with the property, and dealing with serious issues when they arise is much easier. Knowing their market, they believe, can mean seeing opportunities that outsiders might not.

On the other hand, Bruce believes buying in your own suburb is a straight no-no — if your suburb goes off the boil, for whatever reason, not only is the value of your home going to fall, but so too will the value of your investment. Diversification of your property investments is necessary to make sure you don't have all your eggs in the one basket.

Too many Australians break this important rule when it comes to property investment. The temptation to buy an investment property 'just around the corner' from home really should be overcome. If property in your home suburb went through an extended down period, that would be bad enough. But, if your only other major asset was an investment property in that same suburb, you'd be hit twice.

 Diversification doesn't necessarily mean buying on the opposite side of the city to which you live (if you live in a state capital). But it does mean buying somewhere significantly far enough from your home that the direct financial impact of, say, a local major employer going bust would not directly impact on both properties.

For example, if you lived within five kilometres of a major manufacturing plant and the manufacturer went broke, it could take a long time before all those jobs, houses and rental properties that were reliant on the manufacturer remaining in business returned to normal. A local community (or even a large city, as in the case of the collapse of the Pyramid Building Society in Geelong in the early 1990s) can take years to recover from a major economic event.

If, however, you bought an investment property 20 kilometres away from where you lived (and from the manufacturer that went bust), it's unlikely that very many people employed by that company will be living in that part of town. And although it's possible that the reverse could occur — in trying to diversify, you may end up choosing to buy a property in an area where another major manufacturer falls over — the theory is the same. Having a slightly higher risk of losing one egg is better than having a smaller risk of losing all of your eggs.

Across a city or state

Diversification is easily achievable across large cities. If you live in the northern or eastern suburbs of a major state capital, you could investigate suburbs to the south or west that you think are undervalued, and try to find a property that fits your criteria to buy there.

Only five Australian cities have one-million-plus populations. In cities of that size, even if the largest private employer in town collapsed, enough industry exists to keep the impact to less than about 1 per cent of the population. With virtually all other towns in Australia having fewer than 400,000 people, at least one employer would represent 2 or 3 per cent and as much as 5 or 6 per cent of the entire local workforce.

If you live outside a major capital city, consider buying in your state capital to give you the diversification benefits of a big city, particularly as it relates to employment opportunities.

Across Australia

Buying interstate can be advantageous. For a start, you're able to claim against tax a portion of the cost of any trips you make to inspect your investment property, just as you can claim the cost of driving across town to see your investment in your own city.

Australia is a large country with a small population. And it's very rare indeed that the pistons that fire the various economies of this country are firing at the same speed at the same time. Indeed, the term 'two-speed economy' was coined in Australia in 2006 to explain how the 'resource-rich' states of Western Australia and Queensland were experiencing superior economic growth to the non-resource-rich states of New South Wales, Victoria and Tasmania. This was particularly true of property prices. Property prices in Melbourne, Sydney and Brisbane went for a canter between about 1996 and 2003–04. During that time, little out of the ordinary happened with Perth and Adelaide property prices. But during 2005 and 2006, Melbourne and Sydney property prices either tumbled or stagnated, while Perth (and more broadly Western Australian) property prices took off like a rocket, as money poured into the state as a result of the resources boom. Outside of their state capitals, Queensland and South Australian real estate prices showed similar strength on the back of resources.

You can find plenty of opportunities interstate and there may be benefits in regards to land tax (refer to Chapter 7). But you need to spend even more time than normal making sure that all the right research is done, because you won't have a good idea about the suburbs or towns there to start with.

Building an income stream

You make your money from real estate in two ways — through capital gains from the value of the property rising or through having properties that provide a passive income. Of course, you can make your money from a combination of both.

Like actual property prices, rents can stay dormant for long periods. During these times, rents can rise less than inflation for several years, meaning your income is effectively going backwards in the same way that it can go backwards sitting in a low-interest bank account. But, over longer periods, rents would have to rise or there'd be no incentive to buy (either as a home or for investment).

Assuming that the six-strong property portfolio outlined earlier in this chapter had a 4 per cent yield from rent (which is about average for yields in 2013), that portfolio would be producing an income of approximately $284,000 a year by the time the couple were age 65. And, if the rents from those properties rise by 4 to 5 per cent a year, that's a very healthy income indeed.

Part IV
The Part of Tens

Glenn Lumsden

'You tell the kids of today that you didn't get your second investment property till you were 30 and they don't believe you.'

In this part . . .

This part contains a chapter of ten proven ways to enhance the value of a rental property. We touch on topics such as subdividing and developing land to improve value, and also how to improve your management skills. Enjoy!

Chapter 10

Ten Ways to Increase a Property's Return

*A*s we cover through this book, you receive a return on your real estate investments essentially from four basic factors — positive cash flow, equity build-up from paying down your loan, tax benefits and property appreciation. A great aspect of real estate is that the investor can buy properties according to his particular financial and personal needs. Different properties are geared towards achieving more of one of these types of return than another. For example, an investor with significant income from other sources may be able to take the longer term focus that negatively geared properties offer, taking in the tax benefits, and not worry as much about positive cash flow. Investors nearing retirement will prefer properties that create a positive income from day one. And all investors look forward to appreciation (though properties that are negatively geared from day one usually appreciate faster than those that are positively geared from day one).

Successful real estate investors continually ask themselves: How can I improve the returns on my real estate investment in each category? In this chapter, we highlight ten of the best ways you can enhance your return on investment with rental properties.

Raising Rents

Although rental properties may have other sources of income, the largest source is inevitably rent. So real estate investors wisely begin with an understanding that rent increases lead to greater cash flow.

However, setting the weekly or monthly rents and maintaining them at optimum market levels is one of the most common challenges faced by property owners. Many rental property owners are reluctant to raise rents, out of fear they'll lose good tenants. This is a valid concern but shouldn't prevent you from getting rents to market level and maintaining them there — one of the fastest and simplest ways to improve your cash flow. Of course, you should always look for cost-effective ways to improve the property and make sure that your rents are competitive and fair.

We recommend raising the rental rate modestly each year rather than waiting for two or three years and then hitting your tenants with a major increase all at once. Tenants are less likely to move because they understand that the costs of operation rise slightly each year.

If your rents are already at market levels, look to make upgrades to the property to justify higher rents. Maybe the addition of a dishwasher, air conditioning unit, remote control for the garage, an exhaust-vent unit above the stove or the addition of a deck or awning will be an improvement that justifies higher rent. Any improvements that enhance the quality of living or bring the property to a level similar to higher priced properties in the area can justify an increase to the rent being charged, and will probably be a deductible expense, or an item that can be depreciated or claimed as a building cost write-off.

Reducing Turnover

The single most important factor in determining the expenses of most rental properties is turnover of tenants. In both residential and commercial properties, turnover is simply bad for the bottom line. A tenant moving out almost certainly means a loss in rental income (on average, up to three weeks for a residential property, longer for commercial properties), plus you may be hit with some expenses (cleaning, maintenance, repairs and capital improvements) to make the place attractive to show the next prospective tenant. Signing long-term leases with quality tenants, continually maintaining the property in top condition and being responsive to tenant concerns can help reduce turnover, which directly improves the property's profitability.

Another effective tool to reduce the loss of rent when a tenant vacates is to get the premises advertised as being 'available soon' — or 'available from 27 August', for example. As most tenants now first see their new home on the internet (and can elect to receive automatic updates by email), you can almost have your place re-let the first day it's vacant, dramatically cutting your income losses. If you want to show prospective tenants through your property before the current tenant has vacated, make sure you seek permission and give the requisite notice. Also, as soon as you receive a tenant's notice to vacate, immediately seek permission to enter and determine what you need to do to make the property ready for the next tenant.

Subdividing and Developing

Properties on large blocks of land can be perfect candidates for development through subdividing the block and building a second income-producing dwelling. Houses built in the 1950s, 1960s and 1970s in major metropolitan cities in that 'middle ring' out from the CBD were often built on enormous blocks of land (the old quarter-acre block, or bigger). Often, the house was built nearer the front of the land (deliberately to leave a big backyard). In those circumstances, you may have the scope to build a second income-producing house or unit on the back half of the block, with an easement up the side for access, often called a *battleaxe block* because of the shape of the new lot created.

Councils and state governments usually encourage this type of development, because it helps to slow a city's urban sprawl, creates more efficient use of scarce land and adds critical mass for use of local facilities (particularly public transport, schools, hospitals, parks and other council and government-run services). The first port of call for anyone considering any sort of subdivision should be the local council, where you can find out how their process works and what development obstacles you may encounter.

Property development is a different game to property investment and requires a different set of skills. Although investing in real estate is accepted as being at the high end of the risk-and-reward scale, property development is another step up the risk chain. You're betting not only on property, but also on your skills as a project manager, as you try to tie together your planning, organising and negotiating skills for the development of a house. Obviously, the increase in risk comes with the potential increase in reward also.

Keeping Your Banker on Her Toes

Banks need regular reminding that they shouldn't be taking your business for granted. They occasionally need to make you feel special in order to keep you as a satisfied customer. The problem is that banks, like all service providers, don't pay attention to customers who seem to be satisfied (or don't complain), even if they're getting a raw deal. Many customers don't know that they're getting a raw deal. The thinking is that, if the customer isn't whingeing, then he probably isn't unhappy. Those who are in regular contact with their service providers will get a better ongoing deal — 'It's the squeaky wheel that gets the oil'.

You don't have to be on the phone complaining to your bank manager or loan broker every month. But, even if everything is going fine and you're not in touch to complain, you should get on the phone to your personal representative a couple of times a year to find out if she could or should be doing more for you.

Every two years, you should effectively put your banking business out to tender again. Find out exactly what's in your current deal and then go and talk to a mortgage broker to find out how your current deal stacks up against the competition. If it doesn't stack up, you've got two choices. The first is to take the new deal. The second is to go back to your banker and ask him to match it.

Don't let interest rates become the be-all and end-all of your decision to switch lenders. Interest rates are obviously important for real estate investors, but you should also take into consideration the other services your lender provides. Some of the other services (fee-free loans, zero application fees, free credit cards, discounted insurance and so on) may be worth keeping.

Although you can gain significant interest rate discounts by having all your business with the one lender, having two or more banks with parts of your business isn't necessarily wrong. You can play them off against each other as you look to build your portfolio, by asking them to provide their best deal when you look to take out a new loan.

Before signing up for new financing at another lender, always check to make sure that getting out of your current loan isn't going to cost you an arm and a leg in pre-payment penalties. Most loan products nowadays will let you out if you've been with them for a certain period. And in 2011 the federal government banned exit fees with the intention that it would make it easier for borrowers to switch banks. If exit fees apply, find out exactly how much they'll be — you may find switching lenders is still worthwhile, because the lower interest rate at the new lender will pay off the fees and charges within a few months or a year.

Maintaining and Renovating

The kerbside appeal or first impression that your property gives is critical to your overall success. Far and away the easiest way to increase cash flow and increase value is to simply clean up and address the deferred maintenance found in most properties. One of the fundamental rules of real estate is simple supply and demand. If your property really stands out and looks much better than comparable properties, you generate high demand; your rental will stay full at top market rents. That's what cash flow is all about.

Besides attending to the deferred maintenance, another great way to increase cash flow (and value) is to renovate the property. The key here is to spend money only on items that enhance the property and provide a quick payback.

For residential rentals, the best return on investment inside the property is in updating the bathrooms and kitchens. Off-street parking and security measures (such as key-operated locks on ground-floor doors and windows) can also be a positive enhancement in areas where crime is a concern. For commercial properties, upgrading dated interior common areas with higher quality materials and fixtures usually offers the greatest return.

One of the most cost-effective ways to increase the aesthetics and kerbside appeal of any type of property is through landscaping improvements. Often you can simply replace dead plants. If you want to do more, have a landscape architect make suggestions. Whenever you consider these things, be sure to look into the installation of smart ways to conserve water.

Cutting Back on Operating Expenses

One of the first steps to take after you purchase a rental property is to evaluate current operating expenses, with a view to finding room for improvement, particularly without negatively affecting your tenants.

For larger properties, ask the local utility companies for tips to reduce usage. New technology is making the use of solar energy more attractive, and governments have incentives for items like rainwater tanks that can be used for gardening, rather than using town water. Many state governments and councils in Australia have passed laws making it possible (in some states compulsory for new properties) to install individual meters for each dwelling on a property. The rapidly increasing cost of water and sewerage services in many areas of the country may make the installation of individual meters cost-effective for your properties. Large water users who suddenly have to pay for their own consumption often soon learn to conserve a little better.

For larger residential and commercial properties, ask each of the current contractors and service providers to present a proposal or bid for ongoing or new work required. Get some other local companies to provide quotes for the work and ultimately give your business to those firms that offer the best value. As your real estate empire grows, you'll find that contractors and service providers offer discounts based on volume.

Taking Advantage of Tax Benefits

The tax benefits received from real estate vary from investor to investor, but most rental property owners find tax benefits to be a boost to their return.

Even novice real estate investors can take advantage of the generous tax savings with the capital gains exclusion for their principal residence. This exclusion allows vendors to avoid capital gains tax (CGT) on the profit from selling their homes. You can do up your home and sell it for a profit as many times as you like over a lifetime (as long as the ATO accepts that it was your principal place of residence). For investors willing to live in the property during renovation, serial home selling can produce significant tax-free profits (refer to Chapter 2 for this option).

Real estate investors, however, can't escape paying capital gains tax. If an investment property changes beneficial owners, CGT is payable. The good news is that the amount of your capital gain is halved for taxation if you've owned the asset for longer than 12 months.

Depreciation allows the owner to take a non-cash deduction that reduces the investor's taxable income or increases the negative gearing. Land isn't depreciable, so the amount of depreciation is determined by the value of the buildings (built after September 1985) or the value of improvements and contents, as the Tax Office allows most of those items to be written down. Always get a professional (perhaps your accountant could recommend a professional to you) to do a proper depreciation schedule of the property for you. Depreciation deductions are a non-cash item, so they often result in a taxable loss, even if the actual cash flow for the property is positive.

Being Prepared to Move On

When most people think about real estate, they correctly determine that capital appreciation is how the real money is made. Over time, property has proven to be an asset class that increases in value. Even an average annual rate of appreciation of 5 per cent dramatically increases your net worth over time. For an investor with $1 million of property assets, an increase of 5 per cent for a year is $50,000, which is certainly nothing to sneeze at.

However, appreciation can be heavily influenced by outside forces, such as the condition of the suburb, the local community and the local economy. That's why real estate investors need to perform a thorough investigation of an area where an investment is being considered (as we discuss in Chapter 6). But even after you buy a property, you can't simply sit back and let the investment ride as the area deteriorates around you. If the neighbourhood you're in starts to take a downward turn, be prepared to sell and reinvest in a more dynamic area that offers more upside potential.

Adding Value through Change in Use

The entrepreneurial spirit of real estate investors is also rewarded when they're able to increase the return from real estate by adding value through a change in use. A change in use is taking land that isn't currently being used optimally or, as valuers phrase it, for its *highest and best use*, and repositioning the property in a manner that results in the highest value. Several common ways to achieve this are possible, including

- **Improving the land use:** The process of gaining the necessary approvals to put land to a more productive use can take time, but is an extremely powerful way to increase the value of real estate. In nearly every city or town in the country, some land uses, typically agricultural, become less productive (or inadequate) as the area is developed. Taking the steps to get this land approved as residential or commercially zoned property can dramatically enhance property value.

- **Converting use:** The conversion of real estate to another use isn't a new idea, but real estate developers have increasingly practised the concept in recent years. Many other examples of change in use exist: The conversion of apartment blocks to *strata-titled* apartments or units that you can sell individually, or the modification of old warehouses to residential loft apartments and offices.

Improving Management

Management is the one aspect of owning real estate that offers owners an advantage over other types of investments. You can't call Bill Gates and tell him to change Microsoft's products or pricing, even if you do own shares in the company, but superior management of your own rental properties can have a direct impact on your results.

The ability to control and immediately implement different management strategies can lead to more satisfied tenants and longer term tenancies. Some owners are very hands-on with their properties (which we don't recommend for first-time investors or those who aren't prepared to stay on top of current laws — refer to Chapter 8 for more on property management). Others prefer to let a professional handle the day-to-day challenges. A savvy investor knows that the best returns on investment go to owners who have top management. Give your real estate agent a chance if he makes an error (no-one's perfect), but be prepared to sack him and get another manager if you're having to manage the manager too much.

Index

About the Authors

Here are some good reasons we — Bruce Brammall, Eric Tyson and Robert Griswold — believe we're an experienced team of successful real estate investors who have the knowledge to lead you through the property-investment maze.

Bruce Brammall is a licensed financial adviser and mortgage broker, experienced business journalist and finance columnist, bestselling author and successful property investor. As a finance reporter and deputy business editor during his 15 years with Australia's largest selling daily newspaper, the *Herald Sun* — where he got to marry his head for numbers (somewhat rare for a journalist) with writing — Bruce covered the gamut when it came to business and economic issues. He continues to write extensively on property, superannuation, self-managed super funds, shares and the grease that oils property (mortgages and lending) for major media outlets, including News Limited's Australian newspapers (including the *Herald Sun*, the *Daily Telegraph*, *The Courier-Mail*, *The Advertiser*, the *Sunday Times* and *The Mercury*), *Alan Kohler's Eureka Report* and *The West Australian*.

In 2008, he wrote *Debt Man Walking: A 10-Step Investment and Gearing Guide for Generation X* (Wrightbooks). The book launched Castellan Financial Consulting (www. castellanfinancial.com.au), his financial advice business, and, later, Castellan Lending (www.castellanlending.com.au), his mortgage broking business. Prior to that he wrote *The Power of Property: Securing Your Future Through Real Estate*. They were both bestselling titles.

His interest in property began in 1999 when, after reading his first real estate investment book, he decided he wanted to buy his own home. He was talked into delaying that ambition by his now wife, Genevieve, who instead 'let' him buy an investment property. She then 'let' him buy more, and more, one or two of which were homes.

Bruce has a Bachelor of Arts (Communication) with a journalism major (University of Canberra), an Advanced Diploma in Financial Services (Financial Planning) and a Certificate IV in Mortgage Broking. He works in Melbourne as the principal adviser and mortgage broker with, respectively, Castellan Financial Consulting and Castellan Lending.

Bruce and Genevieve live in Melbourne, in an Edwardian work-in-progress, with their children, Ned and Millie.

This book has been adapted by Bruce from the original US edition of *Real Estate Investing For Dummies*, written by Robert Griswold and Eric Tyson. Although the basic principles of property investment are similar the world over, fundamental differences exist between Australia and the United States that affect investment strategies, the seeds of which are sown in the vastly different tax treatments meted out to property investments in each country. Those tax differentials have a cascading effect as they work through the property-investment process.

Eric Tyson is a financial counsellor, lecturer and co-author of the US bestseller *Home Buying For Dummies* (Wiley), as well as the author of four other bestselling US *For Dummies* titles: *Personal Finance, Investing, Mutual Funds* and *Taxes* (co-author). Eric is a devoted financial counsellor and has helped thousands of clients through personal finance, investment and real estate quandaries over the years.

Eric earned his Bachelor's degree in economics at Yale and an MBA at the Stanford Graduate School of Business. Despite these handicaps to clear thinking, he had the good sense to start his own company, which took an innovative approach to teaching people of all economic means about investing and money.

Robert S. Griswold has extensive hands-on experience as a real estate investor working with properties of all types and sizes. He is also the author of the US edition of *Property Management For Dummies* (Wiley) and is a leading columnist and on-air TV and radio presenter in his home state of California.

Robert has been retained on hundreds of legal matters as an expert in the standard of care and custom and practice for all aspects of real estate ownership and management in both state and federal cases throughout the United States. He is the president of Griswold Real Estate Management, managing residential, commercial, retail and industrial properties throughout southern California and Nevada.

Bruce, Eric and Robert are successful property investors in their own right, and write from experience, as well as from the knowledge they have developed from being industry watchers for, collectively, many decades.

Authors' Acknowledgements

Bruce: Ongoing thanks to those in the responsible roles at the time for making my earlier *For Dummies* editions a success, including former John Wiley & Sons general manager Lesley Beaumont, acquisitions editor Charlotte Duff and editor Kerry Davies.

But fitting in time to write a book, around a hectic financial advice and mortgage broking business and family life, is only marginally easier than writing a first edition and not much less daunting. It simply wouldn't have occurred without subtle coaxing from acquisitions editor Clare Weber and project editor Dani Karvess.

Every writer needs editors and I've been fortunate enough to have worked with some very good ones over more than two decades in the craft. Charlotte Duff — back again as editor this time — fits squarely into that category. My sincere thanks go to Charlotte for not just making the editing process headache free, but also improving the book at every turn.

Thanks to co-authors Eric and Robert for providing the original basis for the first edition of *Investing in Real Estate For Dummies* (published in 2008) with the US edition *Real Estate Investing For Dummies* (Wiley, 2005). The book has been essentially rewritten because of the extensive differences between Australian and US tax laws that change many of the fundamentals of property investment strategies between the two countries.

Thanks to my gorgeous wife, Genevieve, for her never-ending encouragement. And for her ongoing permission to take on these projects — they wouldn't be possible without an understanding partner. To my children, Ned and Millie, thanks for making concentration difficult. It's unusually hard to focus with you two around. And you provide the perfect reason to have a break.

To my family (Mum, Dad and Dirk), friends, Castellan clients, colleagues and contacts who, over the years, have extended my property knowledge through their own investment hits and misses.

And, lastly, to former colleague Craig Binnie for throwing me the book that first sparked my obsession with real estate investment. I thank you also for the memorable six-month-long property versus shares argument that followed (though our then colleagues probably don't).

Eric and Robert: Writing a book from scratch is an enormous undertaking, and we couldn't have done it without some invaluable contributions from others. First and foremost we'd like to thank Mike Baker, who worked his magic on each and every chapter, page, paragraph and sentence. He is truly a gifted book editor. We also appreciate the efforts of Jennifer Bingham who did a masterful job as copy editor. And Kathy Cox deserves special praise for believing in us and making this project happen.

Publisher's Acknowledgements

We're proud of this book; please send us your comments through our online registration form located at http://dummies.custhelp.com.

Some of the people who helped bring this book to market include the following:

Acquisitions, Editorial and Media Development

Project Editor: Charlotte Duff, Dani Karvess

Acquisitions Editor: Clare Dowdell

Editorial Manager: Dani Karvess

Production

Cartoons: Glenn Lumsden

Proofreader: Charlotte Duff

Technical Reviewer: Tony Compton

Indexer: Don Jordan, Antipodes Indexing

Want to learn more about property investing?

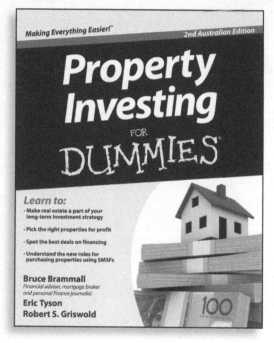

In the book, you'll find:

- Information on using a buyers' advocate

- Tips for owning property with SMSFs

- Help with keeping on top of your paperwork

- How to assemble a reliable support team

Order today! Contact your Wiley sales representative.

Available in print and e-book formats.

Printed in Australia
20 Jan 2017
616154